# SKIING TIPS
## DOWNHILL &
## CROSSCOUNTRY

Rob Hunter & Terry Brown

© COPYRIGHT 1978 AND PUBLISHED BY
COLES PUBLISHING COMPANY LIMITED
TORONTO — CANADA
PRINTED IN CANADA

# CONTENTS

## PART 3: PARALLEL SKIING

# Part 1

# Skiing Basics

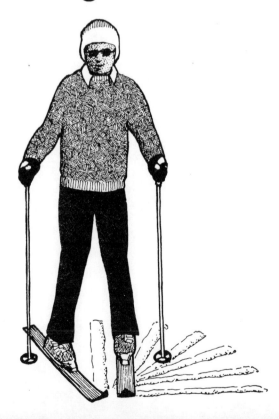

Being older

# INTRODUCTION

## WHY SKI-ING?

Ski-ing is a sport. Many people will say "we're going ski-ing" when what they mean is that they are off to spend a winter holiday in the mountains, lured by such slogans as *"15 days in an Alpine Paradise where King Fun rules supreme"*.

When they get there, they all too frequently find that the holiday is less than enjoyable, parts of it downright scary, and much of it exhausting, especially if their usual idea of exercise is bar billiards, or just getting out of bed in the morning.

Ski-ing, let us say it again, is a sport. To enjoy ski-ing you don't need to be athletic, but it does help to appreciate that like all sports it is more fun if one is fit and ready for all that it entails.

## ABOUT THIS BOOK

This book is not designed to teach you how to ski. It aims to provides a basic introduction to the sport, and tackles in great detail those aspects of the sport that tend to puzzle or discourage the beginner in his first week or two on the snow slopes. It is the first few days that cause the problems, and if they can be overcome, the whole sport becomes easier and, equally important, more fun.

This book, therefore, covers clothing and equipment, where and when to go, getting fit and pre-ski training, boot and ski hire and fitting, ski classes and private lessons, basic snags like climbing, stopping and traversing, ski lifts and slopes, and gives a detailed breakdown of the beginner's main problems.

This book is not designed as a substitute for proper instruction at a good ski school, and under a competent—note competent—instructor. However, if you find certain aspects of the ski-course puzzling, or certain techniques difficult to grasp, then a quiet study of the advice given in this book will be of considerable assistance.

## A FINAL POINT

The ski-ing described in this book, downhill, cross-country, can be found in a score or more countries, in hundreds of resorts, taught by thousands of instructors, to tens of thousands of students.

Within all this there is much variation of opinion, and differences of style and jargon, and some will inevitably disagree with the views and opinions expressed in this book.

We do not pretend that this is the definitive work. We will say that it is sound advice, based on twenty years ski-ing in countries ranging from Japan to Austria, and from the Arctic Circle to the Andes, plus the experience of expert ski-ers and ski-teachers (which is not always the same thing), and lots of helpful hints, and complaints, from the beginners themselves.

If you have any hints for the beginner, write and tell us about them. Suggestions are always welcome, and frequently adopted.

## Chapter 1

## ABOUT SKI-ING
## WHAT, WHERE, AND WHEN TO GO

## WHAT SORT OF SKI-ING

There are basically two sorts of ski-ing. The first is alpine or downhill ski-ing, sometimes referred to as 'piste bashing'. This is most commonly practised in mountain country, and in Europe this usually means France, Italy, Germany, Switzerland and Austria, with new regions being opened up all the time, Spain and the Pyrenees being notable examples.

The other sort is Nordic, langlauf,—'ski du fond'—or cross-country ski-ing, most popular in Scandinavia, notably Norway. The variations between the two types are considerable, since they employ different equipment, and take place over different sorts of terrain. However, it is quite possible, especially in the newer resorts, to try out both sorts of ski-ing, so that opting for the one does not necessarily exclude the opportunity to try the other.

Skiing is practised all over the world, from the Arctic to Australia, and in Europe, from the glens of Scotland to the Sierras of Spain, as well as in the better known Alpine resorts.

## WHERE TO GO

The choice of centre is vast, and as most people, and probably you too, will start ski-ing on holiday, rather than on a specific ski-training course, the choice is yours. You should go for at *least TWO weeks*, if you are to make some progress in ski-ing.

First, get *ALL* the brochures and read them closely. Study the facilities, the terrain, the situation of the slopes, the height, and the day of arrival and departure. Ask advice from anyone who has visited your favoured areas personally.

## FACILITIES

The resort should have a large ski-school, with lots of instructors, preferably with some who speak English, and offering ski-évolutif as well as conventional instruction. You need to note where the nursery slopes are, for they should be within walking distance of the hotels, and not require a time-wasting bus or chair-lift ride to the slopes.

You need to study the terrain, for once you get off the nursery slopes, the beginner needs lots of simple runs to build up his skill and confidence.

Ski runs are graded in colours: Blue (beginners), Red (intermediate), and Black (expert). If the terrain map is seamed with red and black runs, then something less precipitous might be more suitable for a beginner. All brochures *say* that there are facilities for all grades of ski-er, but the map reveals the true picture. Not all brochures have a map, but some do, so see that you get one that does. 'Supertravel' brochures provide excellent terrain maps.

Where the resort itself is, is also important. A six or seven hour coach ride from the airport is boring, tiring, and time-wasting. There are good resorts for beginners within two or three hours of the major airports, Geneva, Zurich, or Milan, and they are worth considering. On the other hand, a resort near a big city will be crowded with visitors at the week-ends.

Then, remember this. Many of the older resorts were Alpine farming communities long before the ski boom began. They were not created as ski resorts, and the ski facilities were built later, sometimes at a considerable distance from the resort itself. On the other hand such villages are attractive, have good hotels, and night life, while the mountains round about have little bars and restaurants that make ski touring very pleasant. Alpbach in Austria is a good example of this sort of resort.

The newer resorts, custom-built for ski-ers, offer excellent ski facilities. The lifts and runs often begin right outside your hotel, and the lift systems are often linked, to hoist you all over the mountains, and they have large, well-staffed ski-schools, teaching all the latest techniques.

On the other hand, they tend to be expensive, having vast investments to recoup, and the night life is limited, while the surrounding hills, if beautiful, are distinctly short of bars.

Personally, as we go for the ski-ing, we prefer the newer resorts, but the choice is yours. As you can see, there are quite a lot of factors to consider with lots of pros and cons, and the more you get right, the more enjoyable your ski-ing will be, when you arrive.

## WHEN TO GO

Ski-ing needs snow. The first snow usually falls in the mountains in November or early December. A ski-resort needs heavy falls in the early weeks, for this snow covers the ground, and the rocks, and provides a deep, firm base for the new snow to fall on later.

This early snow, supplemented by further falls, lasts past the

Christmas high season, through January and February, and well into March. During late February though, the sun gets quite hot in the mountains, hence those much sought-after suntans, and the snow gradually melts in the day, and freezes again at night. Unless there are further falls of fresh snow in March, though, the snow will gradually disappear, and it does so first on the lower slopes, and on the southern faces of the mountains.

## HEIGHT

Now, these remarks are not absolute. The weather varies greatly, and all we would advise you to consider is this. If you are going early or late—say at Christmas or after 1st March, go high, say around 1800 metres (5500 ft.) or higher, or to a resort where the slopes face north. This should ensure that .you have adequate snow without the necessity of travelling far from the resort to find it.

"How's the snow?" is the first question you will hear asked as you get into the coach. On the answer depends your ski-ing. However, even if there is no good snow at your resort, your ski-school will still take you to where the good snow is—but it takes time. Go high, and be more certain. It doesn't mean you will be ski-ing down horrendously steep slopes. It can be just as flat—or as steep up there (on the nursery slopes anyway) as it is down below.

## LOW SEASON OR HIGH SEASON

Ski-ing is expensive (Yes, it is!!) but you can save a great deal by going in the low season, going half-board, and sharing a room. Save your money for the ski-ing.

# Chapter 2

## CLOTHING

So, you have decided to go ski-ing. Fine. Ski-ing, let us repeat, is a SPORT, and like most sports requires the wearing and use of specialised clothing and equipment.

From the feet up, consider the following (Figure 1):

1. Socks: For ski-ing you need a thin or medium pair of wool socks to wear next to the skin plus (perhaps) a thicker pair over the top. If you wear woollen tights, as we do, then you don't need the thin socks. Wear as few socks as possible. In the old days with leaking leather boots you needed two pairs of socks to keep your feet warm, but modern boots are warm and waterproof, and you don't want your feet, which control your skis, swaddled in unwieldly thick socks. Feet sweat (sorry!) (but they do) so you will need three pairs, one on, one off, one in the wash!

2. Tights: I have a pair of black wool tights, which I bought in Austria in 1957. They are referred to by my friends as 'Rob's Diagalievs'. Jeer if they must, but my L.J.'s keep me and my leg muscles warm, and a warm muscle will stretch, where a cold, stiff one will wrench. We will not labour the point about tights, but we think they are a worthwhile investment. Buy wool, not nylon, for it's warmer, and wool creates no friction against the nylon lining of the boot. For the same reason nylon tights will not do.

3. Boots: Boots are so important in ski-ing that they are hardly clothing at all. They are, therefore, covered on Page 17 under equipment.

4. Trousers: There are various types of trouser, or to be more exact, types of trouser bottom. Go for the wide bottom type of stretch pants. The type that clip to the boot are no use for anything other than ski-ing, and for the beginner, who may not take to the sport, they are an unnecessary frill, while the ski-overall, or Salopette, is better bought when you are quite sure you will go ski-ing regularly. One pair of stretch pants will be sufficient.

5. Sweaters: You should take with you a few cotton roll-neck shirts and light sweaters, far the most useful and therefore the most popular wear for the upper body, is the cotton roll-necked sweater, worn with a V-necked lambswool or oiled wool sweater, and an anorak. Sweaters get sweaty, so take

FIGURE 1

several. It can get very hot on the ski-slope, so don't assume that only heavy thick gear need be taken. Three roll-necked cotton sweaters, two light V-necked wool pullovers, and one heavy wool one, is about right. Make sure they are long, the longer the better.

6. Anoraks: Again there is a wide choice. The ideal ski anorak should be hip-length, fit closely at the waist, neck and wrists, and have lots of zipped pockets. Zips should be covered with flaps and popdown studs. The anorak can be any colour you like, but check that the material is 'anti-glis', that is, of a material that tends to stop you sliding when you fall, rather than lets you slip (or glissade) away down the slope. I fell once in Austria, and slid head-first on my back, over fifty yards down a very steep slope, losing skis, hat and goggles, quite unable to stop. It was very perturbing, and my ski-ing anorak was largely to blame. So, ask for 'anti-glis' material if you are buying a new anorak. Your old or present one may do for your first time ski-ing, but check with a knowledgeable friend or the local ski-shop first.

7. Head-gear: The body loses 30% of its heat through the head, so wear a hat. You need one that will keep the ears warm, and help keep your sunglasses on. A wool hat (preferably without a bobble) is the neatest and best.

8. Gloves: Gloves or mittens? Mittens are warmer, but you will often have to take them off, and then your hands get wet and cold. Better buy a loose-ish pair of ski-gloves and wear a woollen pair inside if necessary. They should cuff over the cuffs of the anorak, and fit closely at the wrists. *NEVER* ski without gloves.

9. Ski-glasses or Goggles: Really you need both. Ordinary sun-glasses are quite good enough for all normal purposes, but if it is snowing, or you are doing a long, cold, downhill run, put the goggles on. When not in use, just slide them up on their strap around your upper arm.

10. Après-ski clothing: While you hear a lot of talk about dancing in ski-boots, and staying in the same gear all day, you'll probably want to change in the evening. You won't need an out-door jacket, your anorak will do, but take warmish trousers, and above all, sensible shoes. No leather soles. If you nip out at night, you'll be nipping across ice and frozen snow and can come a very nasty cropper. If you have a use for them elsewhere, buy a pair of 'moon boots', but no thin-soled city shoes, whatever you wear.

## IMPORTANT

A final point: Ski-ing is a casual sport, and no great range of glamour gear is necessary. Remember that specially from mid-February on, it can be very warm out there, especially when flogging around on the nursery slopes. On the other hand, you can get very cold indeed in mist on a chair lift, or a long tow. The secret is to have a few layers of clothing, which you can put on, or peel off, as the day or situation demands. Tie sweaters round your waist, or put them in a 'bum bag' when not in use.

Chapter 3

## EQUIPMENT
## BOOTS, BINDINGS, SKIS AND POLES

### BOOTS

The most important piece of equipment is the boot. Boots transmit your intentions from the foot through the binding to the ski. With ill-fitting boots you will find ski-ing difficult, and probably very uncomfortable. Ill-fitting boots, which cause sore feet or ankles put more people off ski-ing than anything else, so:

**GET GOOD FITTING BOOTS, WHATEVER YOU DO**

Change them again and again until they do fit, no matter how long it takes. 'Flow-fit' boots, which have a padded lining that adjusts to your foot when warm, are very suitable.

### CHOOSING YOUR BOOTS

Get hold of a ski boot and examine it. Nowadays boots are made from plastic, have a hard outer shell, and a soft, padded, removable liner, a long tongue, and do up with clips. They are often hinged at the ankle. Examine your boots and clips carefully (Figure 2).

To get the boots right, proceed as follows. (We assume a 4-clip boot.)

1. Ask the assistant for your normal shoe size. Metric sizes are (approximately) as follows:

   | Old-Style | 6 | 7 | 8 | 9 | 10 | 11 |
   |---|---|---|---|---|---|---|
   | Metric | 38 | 40 | 42 | 43 | 44 | 45 |

   Whatever your actual size is doesn't matter. You want boots that fit, but by asking for your normal shoe size you get into the right size area. Wear your ski socks.
2. Undo the clips completely, and pull out the tongue towards the boot toe.
3. Put the foot into the boot endeavouring to press your heel back into the rear of the boot. 'Flow-fit' boots take time to warm up and adjust to your foot.
4. Fold back the tongue neatly, and do up the bottom clips, to grasp the foot firmly, but **not** tightly. Do the same with the top clip, leaving the middle one, if any, undone.
5. Stand up.
6. Your big toe is probably touching the front of the boot. Unless it is pressing hard enough to be uncomfortable, this is all right.

FIGURE 2

7. Now, keeping the heels of the boots on the ground, and looking down, flex the knees forward, over the toes of the boots.
Your heels should now slip back into the heel of the boot,
and your toes ease off the front. If this happens, the fit is
probably all right. The toes should be able to wriggle.

8. Still keeping the knees flexed as far forward as possible, bend
down or get a friend to do up the third clip, if any, as tightly
as possible. This is the clip that clamps your heel into the
rear of the boot, and keeps it there. For good ski-ing *THE*

*HEEL MUST NOT RISE*—remember that. You probably now feel—what a rigmarole! Quite so, but comfortable, well-fitting boots can make or break your holiday, and make the difference between becoming a good ski-er and retiring miserably to the bar. So, read this section several times until you are certain you will know how to try on a pair of ski boots. They will feel very stiff and strange, like deep-sea divers' boots, but those are your feet in there, and only you can decide, from the above information, if you have a good fit.

Now for some final points:

(a) Most beginners wear boots that are TOO BIG. It's the most common fault, so watch out for it.

(b) Your own shoe size is only a guide. Get boots that *fit*, not your usual $8\frac{1}{2}$.

(c) Ski boots are for ski-ing, not for walking. When you are not flexing, the toes should touch the front.

(d) When flexed, and clipped up, the heels should be held firmly down, the toes just off the front, and the toes free to wriggle.

(e) We have assumed for this book that your boots have four clips, but they can have any number. Just be sure that when the clips are done up *the heel does not rise*.

(f) The padded tongue fits comfortably over the shin.

## HIRE OR BUY, HOME OR ABROAD

We have taken a lot of advice on this, and the general concensus of opinion is that the beginner should **hire** his boots **at home**, and hire them a week before he goes ski-ing.

There are a number of reasons for this. If you hire at home, it is likely that you and the fitting assistant will have more time, and can use it to get good fitting boots. The ski-shop abroad, when a group arrives, is a shambles, and the urge is to settle for any pair of boots and skis and get out of the crowd and on to the slopes. Hiring at home saves time out there, as you only have to fit skis.

But the biggest advantage is that it gives you a chance to wear the boots around the house and see if they fit—*really* fit. Which brings us to our last tip. If you are going on a two week holiday, as you should, hire the boots a week early, to check the fit. You can wear them for your pre-ski exercises, and really get used to them, and *change them* if they prove uncomfortable.

Incidentally, don't be put off by some ski shops refusal to hire for three weeks (the most vocal snag we ran into). They will hire for one week, or two weeks, and when we were lads 1 + 2 = 3.

Finally, again, if your boots don't fit, or are paining you, change them as often as it takes, until you solve the problem. The new boots may not rub you in the same place as the previous pairs.

## SORE ANKLES
If your ankles are swollen and sore, get the boots off, and soak the ankles, or use cold compresses until you reduce the swelling. Then strap the area with adhesive tape. Don't use more padding or extra socks, that simply increases pressure on the sore area. If it's really bad you may, apart from fresh boots, need to stop ski-ing for a day. That's why a two-week holiday is best. It gives you time for rest and recovery.

## POLES
Ski-sticks are more correctly known as poles. As they are the simplest bit of equipment, we will dispose of them before going on to skis and bindings.

The correct length of the pole is when you can hold it, tip sunk in snow, with the forearm at right angles to the body. The best way to judge this is to hold the pole upside down, by the spike below the basket. If the butt rests on the ground and the forearm is straight, the pole is the right length.

Do hold the poles correctly. Study the diagram (Figure 3) and note that the strap goes over the back of the hand, which then grasps the straps and handle. Don't have your pole-straps flapping.

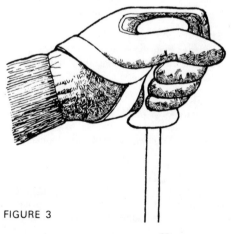

FIGURE 3

23

## SKIS

It would be quite easy to write a whole book on skis, and ski-lore. However, let us stick to basics, in which you will find three main types of ski.

1. Short skis, in varying lengths, for ski-évolutif.
2. Compact skis.
3. Conventional skis.

## SHORT SKIS

If you are learning on ski-évolutif, you will use skis starting about 1 metre (39 inches) long, and proceed, increasing the length of the ski as your skill develops, up to your correct length. The training will be done under the guidance of your instructor, and the method of instruction and length of ski are so closely linked as to remove the choice from the beginners' hands.

## COMPACT SKIS

Compact skis are rarely over 180 cms in length, and are wider than the conventional ski. The normal length for men lies between 170 cms—180 cms, and for women between 150 cms and 170 cms ($2\frac{1}{2}$ cms = 1 inch approx.).

When you hire skis, you **may** be offered a choice between compact and conventional skis. If so, choose the compacts. Usually you will be offered only compact skis.

They are, as we have noted, shorter and wider than the conventional ski, and are generally more suitable for the beginner, for controlled ski-ing on firm piste or over 'mogul' slopes.

## CONVENTIONAL SKIS

These are narrower and longer than the compact. They can go up to 210 cms and are excellent for fast running, on off-piste snow, and for fast tight turns.

## WHAT LENGTH OF SKI?

For the last ten years, the trend of opinion has been for the ski length : skiers' height ratio to get less. People skied on ever shorter skis and this led, eventually, to the development of évolutif.

At present the trend is reversing itself slightly, and longer skis are becoming more fashionable again.

You must ski on skis that are right for you, and your height is only one, and the least important factor in the choice. It used to be held that the correct length was judged when you stood with

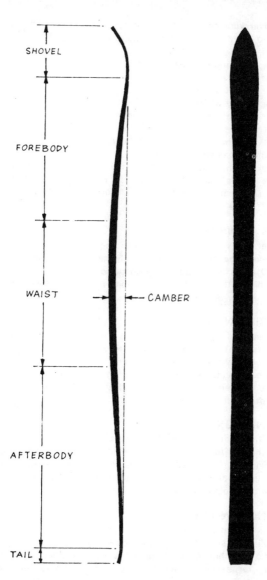

FIGURE 4

your hand over your head, and the correct length ski was the one where the tip fitted into the palm of the upheld hand. This was a very long ski, by present standards.

To get the right length of ski, consider:
1. Your height.
2. Your weight and build.
3. Your degree of fitness.
4. Your ski-ing experience and skill.

The taller, heavier, fitter and more experienced you are, the longer the ski. If you are a short, thin, asthmatic dart player, then your skis will be somewhat minute.

Study the lengths for men and women (Page 21), and considering the points just covered, go for the longer or shorter length. The ski length, in centimetres, is cut into the side of the ski.

## BINDINGS (Figure 5)

Bindings are a very critical piece of equipment, and the choice is wide. However, the beginner will usually have the choice made for him, and again, there are only two basic areas, not counting:

**Cable Bindings:** If you are offered 'cable' bindings, refuse them. Pay more for better bindings if necessary. Get:

## STEP-IN BINDINGS

The toe of the binding is usually fixed on a swivel, while the heel-plate rises. You put the boot toe into the toe of the binding, step down and the heel-plate clicks down and shut. To release, you usually depress a catch in the heel-plate. In a fall, with a 'step-in' binding, the toe releases sideways, and the heel-plate rises, to free the boot.

## PLATE BINDINGS

With these the boot is fixed to a flat-plate and the plate in turn, is fixed to the ski. In a fall, the whole plate slips away from the ski. Plate-bindings, which allow the boot to release under any strain, are highly recommended. Their release qualities are superior to step-in or cable bindings.

## ADJUSTING BINDINGS

The bindings should be tight enough to stay on for hard ski-ing, and easy falls, but should come off at once if you take a real spill.

If you find your binding releasing while you are doing a snow plough turn, for example, then it is too loose. If you come a

STEP IN BINDING

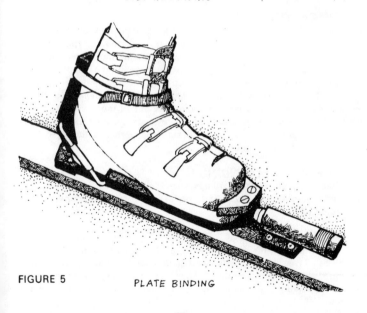

FIGURE 5　　　　PLATE BINDING

27

cropper and your skis stay on, then they are too tight, and may need to be eased. Most bindings have a dial or grid, which indicates where the correct fit (for your boots) should be. Note this as you leave the fitting bench, and if you see the mark has moved, check the binding, and have them adjusted if necessary.

Bindings can freeze. If you take the skis off at lunchtime, snap the bindings a few times before you put the skis on again, especially if the day is cold, foggy or icy.

## SKI STRAPS OR SKI-STOPPERS

Your bindings should have straps. Then, if you fall, your skis will stay with you. This is nice for you, as you can put them on again, and nice for everyone else, as a runaway ski hitting someone can cause severe injuries, for which incidentally, the person who let the ski go is liable in law. Besides, you probably won't be able to ski on one ski only, and it's a long way down!

Many modern bindings incorporate 'ski-stoppers', little prongs held down by the foot when in the binding, but springing down to stop the ski running when the foot is released.

You must have one or the other, and preferably both.

## CHECK YOUR SKIS

When you are handed your skis take a good look at them. They must have safety bindings of the 'plate' or 'step-in' type and look in reasonable condition. Check that the metal edges are complete, and run your thumb gently along the edge of the metal runners. If they are completely rounded you may not be able to 'edge' your skis into hard snow or ice. Ski edges can be sharpened, so if they are quite round and smooth, point this out to the assistant.

Hire skis do get quite a bit of hard wear, so don't expect to get new glittering models. Just be sure they are not damaged, and that the edges are complete.

## CHECK YOUR BINDINGS

Toe, heel, and plate bindings should release, *with difficulty*. Try and move them, and if it's too easy or impossible, have them adjusted.

## BITS AND PIECES

In the pocket of your anorak you should carry a few odds and ends. Two handkerchiefs are useful, one for blowing your nose, and wiping your streaming (from the cold air) eyes; the other for cleaning glasses and goggles. Take a lip-salve. Take some chewing gum, you'll get thirsty. If you carry money, don't carry it in your trouser pockets. A fall onto your pocket can leave the Austrian eagle, or the Swiss cross bruised into your flank for days. If you carry a tube of sun cream, don't land on it, it makes a frightful mess.

Wax: A piece of silver wax is useful. You may find that your skis won't move, or that snow is balling up underneath. A rub of silver wax along the bottom will cure the problem.

Ski-clips: These are little rubber straps, with snap hooks on the end, to hold the skis together when carting them about. They are most useful, but easily lost, so the ski hirers don't lend them any more. Buy four—you will need two, and are bound to lose one so . . .

## HIRE OR BUY?

Hire your skis initially, and hire them abroad. Then if anything breaks you can go back to the hire shop and get another pair. Your insurance, or the holiday tour insurance, should cover the breakage. Skis and bindings are expensive, and until you are going to ski regularly, buying skis is unnecessary. Anyway, your first major purchase of equipment should be boots.

## Chapter 4

## GETTING FIT AND PRE-SKI EXERCISES

Ski-ing is a sport. You will enjoy it more, find it easier, and be less tired, if you get fit, or at least fitter, before you go. If your idea of exercise is getting out of bed in the morning, then your first few days on the slopes will prove a traumatic experience.

Getting fit is perhaps more important for the beginner than for the more experienced ski-er. The beginner uses fewer lifts, does more climbing on skis, and being inexperienced, puts unnecessary effort into his ski-ing.

The bulk of this work falls on the legs, torso, and back, so our exercises are designed to strengthen these areas particularly.

### THE LEGS

The best exercise for the legs is to use them, so: *walk, jog,* or *run.*

**Walk** hard, don't stroll. Walk uphill forcing the legs to drive against the slope. Coming down the hill, *JOG.*

**Jogging** downhill is very good for the calf muscles, and the knee joints. Short, pounding, controlled steps will test these muscles, without overstraining them. Walk uphill, and jog down.

**Run.** Running is an excellent exercise, for it strengthens the legs and builds up stamina.

In the evening, go for a run. It doesn't matter how far, but the longer the better, provided you don't overdo it. Wear *boots* or *heavy shoes*, not track shoes or gym-shoes. You will be wearing ski boots, remember, and your legs need to get used to the idea of exercising with a weight on the end. Don't, however, go running in your ski boots.

You can exercise the legs by standing on them, so stand—don't sit, on buses or trains. Use stairs, not lifts or escalators, and always use the legs **hard.** Put some beef into it! Now for a few exercises. Do these daily, for three weeks before you go.

### HIGH STEPS

This is one for home or office, and you need a strong chair, a bench or a low wall, ideally just over knee-height. Do this exercise in your ski boots once you have hired them.

The exercise is quite simple: (1) You put one foot on the chair and step up onto it. (2) Step down and put the other foot up, and step up onto the chair again. (3) Continue, left foot, right foot, until you can't go on any longer. Repeat regularly, during the day. This exercise is very good for the whole leg, ankles, calves, knees, thighs and hips. Do this exercise anywhere, home or office, three times a day for at least three weeks before you go (Figure 6).

## LEG RAISING

A good one for the office chair or while watching television. Sitting comfortably put a weight of some sort, a briefcase or a small pillow stuffed with books to weigh about 3 kilos (say 7 lbs.) across the ankles, or supported in a basket or shopping bag. (1) Raise the legs, until they are level with the knees. (2) Now lower. (3) Repeat. Do this exercise *slowly*. The strain will fall in the muscles behind the knees, and the thighs. You can do this at any spare moment (Figure 7).

## SQUAT SITS

Very simple, very effective, and good for the balance. Stand, legs and feet together, arms by the side. (1) Keeping the heels on the floor, sit down slowly until you are squatting on your heels. Don't use the arms at all. (2) Now stand up, slowly. Repeat until you can't! (Figure 8).

## STRIDE JUMPING AND HOPPING

(1) Start arms at side, legs together. (2) Then stride-jumping, legs apart, arms to shoulder-height, spring on the toes, the arms slapping the thighs as the feet come together. Vary this by hopping on one leg, raising the other to the side, the arms held steady at the sides. This is a nice lively exercise to warm you up (Figure 9).

## ANKLES

Rocking: Feet together, arms at the side. Rock the feet from side to side, flexing the ankle to put the weight on the side of the foot. A good exercise for 'edging', and best done in ski boots or shoes.

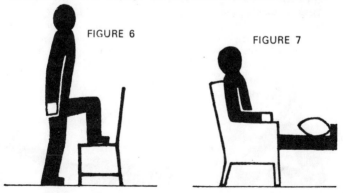

FIGURE 6          FIGURE 7

FIGURE 8    FIGURE 9

## TRUNK EXERCISES

The muscles that will take the pounding are in the back, stomach and abdomen. Anything you can do to strengthen them will be beneficial.

## SIT-UPS

(1) Lie flat on the floor, arms at the side. Start by raising the head until you can see your knees, then lower. Keep it up until stomach muscles scream. (2) Same start position. This time sit up until you are upright—now lower. Repeat. Continue until gasping. Try and touch the legs, as far down as possible, with the finger tips. If you can touch the toes without flexing the knees— congratulations! (Figure 10).

These two exercises strengthen muscles above the belt. For those below, try the following:

## LEG RAISING

Same starting position: (1) Raise the feet slowly until you can see the ankles. (2) Now, slowly, lower. (3) Repeat. Your stomach muscles will soon complain. Keep going. Vary this by raising the feet, then slowly opening the legs, then feet together, then down. The slower you can do this the better (Figure 11).

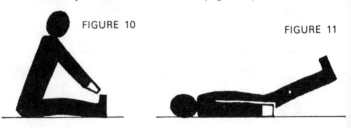

FIGURE 10    FIGURE 11

FIGURE 12

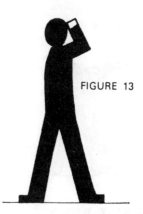

FIGURE 13

## BICYCLING

Raise the legs in the air, then keep them there by propping the hips with the hands, elbows spread. Now cycle (Figure 12). This strengthens the leg and stomach muscles and gets you puffing.

## BACK EXERCISES

Good posture is the best thing for the back, and bad posture the cause of most back complaints. The muscles in the back need to be flexible.

## TRUNK TWISTING

(1) Stand erect, feet apart, hands behind the head, fingers linked. (2) Turn the trunk sharply until the left elbow points to your front, then back. (3) Now right elbow. (4) Repeat. Force the body round, flexing the waist and back muscles eight to ten times each way (Figure 13).

## TOE-TOUCHING

(1) Stand upright, legs apart, arms outstretched. (2) Now bend smoothly to touch left toe with right hand, and up. (3) Now down again, right toe with left hand, and up. (4) Repeat (Figure 14).

Always come up completely, and pause between movements. Assume good posture, back straight and hollow, shoulders square, head erect, tummy in, chest out.

As you get better, try touching the toes with the feet together, a straight down and up, pause, down and up. Don't flex the knees.

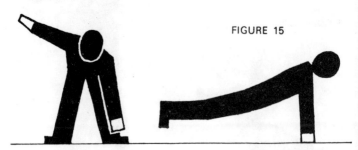

FIGURE 14

FIGURE 15

## SQUAT JUMPS
Crouch down, knees apart, weight on toes, and resting on the knuckles of the fist. The exercise consists of throwing the legs back and forward, as far and as fast as possible. Keep it up as long and as fast as possible. Work hard! (Figure 15).

## ARM EXERCISES
The upper arms and shoulders get used, especially in climbing. Press-ups, or pull-ups, in groups of ten, will stretch and strengthen arm and shoulder muscles.

## HOW TO EXERCISE
Exercising is BORING. That's why people don't keep it up for long. To be effective you must exercise for twenty minutes a day every day, and it can become very, very boring.

So try to exercise in a group. Get your ski party together for a run, or to go swimming. Do the exercises with the family. If on your own, put on an L.P. record, and run through the exercises once to one side, and once to the other, And make your body *WORK*.

## A FINAL POINT ON FITNESS
You don't need bulging muscles, you need firm, flexible, supple ones. Get them used to being used, especially over the three weeks before you go. While it would be best for everyone if we exercised all the time, to get the best from your ski-ing, try and get fit by exercising your body in the *three* weeks before you go. Don't overdo it to begin with.

## PRE-SKI CLASSES AND ARTIFICIAL SKI-ING

There are sure to be pre-ski classes available near your home. As soon as you have booked your holiday, book some pre-ski lessons. Even if these are just exercises held in a ski-shop or gym, they are worth while.

You will learn how to fit boots and skis, how to hold the poles, how to turn on skis, and you can make, and learn from, a lot of trivial mistakes. You can also pick up a lot of background knowledge from your instructors and class-mates.

## ARTIFICIAL SKI-ING

Artificial ski-slopes are small, usually man-made hills, covered with a type of stiff plastic matting. There is an artificial ski-ing syllabus, and a laid-down course of instruction for teaching all grades of ski-er on artificial slopes, and the courses cover much of the ground that you will cover later, on real snow during your holiday. So if an artificial course is available, please take it.

One point is recommended. When you book your holiday, you should have noticed if the centre you are going to, offers ski-évolutif. If so, do you intend to take it? We think you should, and this being the case, try and take évolutif classes on the artificial slope too, if possible.

Incidentally, when you get to the snow, don't argue with Hans, or Pierre, or Mario, that Bill, back on that matting-covered garbage dump in Canada knows better than he does. Bill may, but it's best to keep quiet about it. Also, when you join another ski class, don't say what you can *do*, say what you have *done*. The instructors will find out what you can do, for themselves, very quickly. But do go artificial ski-ing if you can, you'll find it helps enormously when you get on to real snow.

## Chapter 5
## SKI LIFTS AND SKI RUNS

Quite a lot of people dislike ski-lifts intensely. In any resort there is usually at least one lift that the beginners, and quite probably everyone else is very wary of. But lifts are a fact of life on the ski slopes; most of them are very easy, and if you are to enjoy your ski-ing to the full, all need to be mastered.

We will start with the least familiar and least difficult and work our way up.

## CABLE CARS

A number of resorts, especially in Switzerland, have ski areas that can only be reached by cable car. This is no more difficult than entering a Tube-train. You enter the station, pay for your ticket, and go along a ramp into the gondola, the doors close and off you go. They sway a bit, and if you have no head for heights don't look out of the window.

## CHAIR LIFTS

These are very common, and take the ski-er up to the high slopes. you will surely be using chair lifts in your second week, if not before, and there are various points to bear in mind. Remember that chair lift rides can be long and cold, so wrap up well before you get on. Some resorts will even lend you a rug.

Usually, though not invariably, you wear your skis, but be prepared to take them off and carry them. Most chair lifts carry two, but sometimes three people. You are expected to get on when it is your turn, and not hang back or push forward to stay with your chums.

Sometimes two chair lifts, or tows, leave from the same station. Don't, in the melée, at the bottom, get on the wrong lift and lose your class.

## COPING WITH CHAIR LIFTS

Much of this advice holds good for all lifts, tows and drags. If they are new to you, or of an unfamiliar type, first go to the side where you can see people getting on, and watch the routine. See how the pairs move forward, where they stand, what they do with poles and skis, and where the *safety bar* comes over. Most chair lifts have a *safety bar* which, once you are seated and away, is pulled down over your head, to hold you in place. They usually have a little bar to rest your boots and skis on. Have a good look, then, before you join the queue.

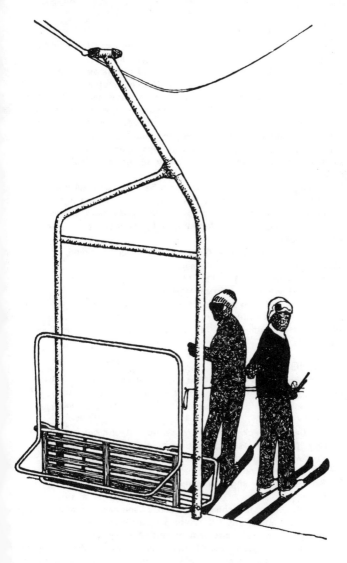

FIGURE 16

37

## GETTING ON

Take your hands out of the pole straps, get your pass or ticket ready, if not already visible, and join the queue.

When you get to the front, you will find two people already out on the ramp waiting for their chair. Notice (1) that the ends of their skis are resting at a wooden step in the snow to stop them slipping back. (2) They are holding their poles in the inside hand. (3) They are looking back over their outside shoulders, probably holding their outside hand out ready to grasp the chair (Figure 16).

Round comes the chair, the seat bumps against their knees, they sit down smartly, and are borne away, lowering the safety bar as they go.

As soon as they are away, don't hesitate, get out there! Go forward then slip back until the ski ends are resting against the wooden bar, transfer both poles to the inside hand, if you have needed both poles to get forward, and look round over your outside shoulder.

This may be done in a flurry, but you will soon find that you have plenty of time, so don't panic.

As the chair comes round, reach for it and as it bumps your knees, sit down. Keep your ski tips up.

You may find that as the chair moves off it sways about, so just stay seated until you are a few yards up the line, and then get organised, and lower the safety bar. Settle down and enjoy the ride.

## GETTING OFF

After a while you will see that people ahead of you are getting off. One pylon from the top, lift the safety bar. What happens at the top may vary, but it does pay to prepare for the dismount as follows.

1. Get the feet back, keeping the ski tips up, and get your bottom forward, the poles held, as before, in the inner hand.
2. You will be sitting quite close to the ground as you run over the top ramp and may need the poles to lever yourself up.
3. Ski away at an angle from the chair, one left, one right, transferring the poles to each hand and coming to a stop. Don't stop too near the chairs, as other people will be flooding off after you, and if you fall, try to get out of their way.

**One tip:** If, in the excitement of getting away, you drop a pole, don't worry, and don't fall off the chair snatching after it. When you get to the top, hang about, and someone will bring your pole up for you within a few minutes.

If you drop it down some abyss on the way up, then you have a problem, but you usually get your pole back in the end. The same holds good if you drop a pole on a drag lift. Someone will bring it up for you, so don't fall off and stop the whole line unnecessarily.

## DRAG LIFTS

There are usually two sorts. The T-bar is generally for two people, and the 'button' lift for one. They are used for the short and medium length tows, which can be up to a mile in length.

In both cases the bars circulate on a moving cable, and the 'button' or T-bar is suspended on a spring-loaded pole and cable.

## T-BARS

As they are designed for two people, try and get on with someone else. Try also to get on with someone your own height. I spent a morning once going up and down with a group of children. I am 6 ft. tall, and crouching down so they could get their much lower bottoms on the bar fairly wore me out! If you are on your own don't put one of the short T-arms between your legs and go that way. Sit on one side, its safer.

FIGURE 17

## GETTING ON

As with the chair lift, have a look first and observe the routine. Get ticket, gloves and poles organised before you join the queue.

When it is your turn, ski forward, let the back of the skis rest against the wooden stop bar (if any). Be sure: (1) Your skis are parallel, and (2) your poles are in the outside hand (the long arm of the T-bar will come on the inside, between the two of you). (3) Both look back over your inward shoulder and, as the T-bar approaches grab it and tuck the T under your seat(s). Don't sit down! If you do you'll fall over as the spring loaded wire reels out (Figure 17).

After you have positioned the T-bar, there will be a slight pause, while the wire takes up the slack. Keep your knees slightly bent, until with a jerk, hard or soft, you are off.

Frequently you move off with a jerk, then slow or stop again, and as you almost overbalance, there is another jerk and you are finally away. That is why we suggest you study the ski-ers in front, and see if the drag has any little surprises.

On the way up, keep the skis parallel and ride easily in the tram lines made by the previous ski-ers. Keep leaning back against the T-bar so that there is a steady pressure easing you up the slope. If the tow stops—usually because someone has fallen off and is causing a traffic jam behind, just rest, easy but alert, until you start moving again.

## GETTING OFF

If you are on with a stranger, and you don't speak the same language, establish by grins, nods and pointing who will get off first, and who will dispose of the T-bar.

Don't get off too soon. Wait till you are up on the flat, and the first off skis out of the way, while the second holds the long arm of the T-bar and lets it go under control.

Don't just let the bar fly off. If the T hooks in your anorak, or round the pole straps, it can cause you injury. Let it go gently.

## BUTTON LIFTS

These work on the same principle as the T-bar, but instead of a T-bar you have a little metal seat which you place between your legs (Figure 18).

Button lifts don't usually circulate on an endless belt, but are gathered into a bunch at the start of the lift, and started by a switch.

FIGURE 18

You get your tow by (1) waiting until the previous ski-er has gone, (2) a bar across your front will drop, and you slide forward, poles in the outer hand, tripping a little spring with your knees, (3) this spring activates a switch, and your 'button' lift slides forward. Seize it with your nearside hand, tuck the seat under your bottom, and off you go. The dismount is in your own hands, so just be careful.

All this apart, the best advice is to study the lift before you attempt to get on it. See how the others do it, watch for snags, get organised and DON'T WORRY.

## SKI RUNS

So, having mastered the lifts and tows, you arrive at the top. People are taking off in all directions, and there is a choice of runs. Which way do you go?

Ski runs are graded into degrees of difficulty:

> BLUE — for beginners
> RED — for intermediates
> BLACK — for experts

Poles with discs in these colours will mark the appropriate run. This degree of difficulty is averaged out over the run, so you can find easy spots on a black run, and difficult ones on a red run. As a beginner you should follow the class, or stick to the blue runs.

A few little rules for when you are on the run might be mentioned here. Don't stop in the middle of the run, go to the side of the piste. It is the overtaking ski-er's responsibility to avoid running down the one in front.

Don't go sailing over anything or go racing round a corner when you don't know what is on the other side. Finally, if you see a line of crossed slalom poles barring your path, stop, and seek another way. This indicates danger. Don't assume that you will find crossed poles only on the edge of cliffs. The snow may have melted on the piste exposing rocks, and you don't want to run into those!

# Chapter 6

## SKI CLASSES AND PRIVATE LESSONS
## BOOKING CLASSES, EQUIPMENT AND PASSES

We recommend that your first ski-ing holiday should be for at least fourteen days, and that you should book for two weeks of lessons, but pay for only a one-week lift-pass.

There are several points to consider here.

You will, for a start, need to have lessons and hire skis and poles. If you do this at home you can pay in sterling, and obtain some financial advantage from the travel agent's block-booking arrangements with the hire shops. For equipment and classes then, hire for the whole period and pay at home. Your trip should be for two weeks, so that you really get the hang of ski-ing, and can have a day off if you feel like it, or get over-tired.

Lift-passes are a different matter. It is not likely that you will initially use many of the longer lifts, and lift passes are expensive. You can, at the resort, buy single tickets, and possibly buy a pass or 'abonnement' for the range of lifts you are actually using. To spend money on an over-all pass for the whole lift system is a waste of money. At most, buy a complete pass for the second week. Remember to take two or three passport size photos with you for the pass tickets.

## GETTING ORGANISED

As soon as you arrive discover the location of (1) The ski hire shop. (2) The ski school office and assembly point. (3) Where they issue lift tickets or passes.

You might care to organise (2) and (3) while the rest are crushed into the ski shop. Get your ski-lesson voucher exchanged for lesson tickets, and find out where the classes meet. Find someone who has been there a week and get some tips on the daily routine and night life.

On the first morning get to the assembly point early, and seek out an instructor who can understand you. Tell him what ski-ing or pre-ski-ing or artificial ski-ing you have done, and he will direct you to a group. Don't say what you can **do,** say what you have **done.** You may have to demonstrate your ability in a short test.

Ski-ing skills are graded numerically. In Switzerland, they go from Group 1 (absolute beginners), to Group 6 (the experts). In France and Austria it is the other way round, you start at Group 6 and end up a marvel in Group 1.

Within each group there will be several classes, and although they follow the same syllabus, one class may be more advanced than another, because those in that class are making faster progress.

If you have been to dry-ski classes and done some artificial skiing, you may find the basic beginners class just too basic for you. If so, get out of it. Many people, the nicer ones in fact, are happy to just stay with the group, but ski-lessons are expensive, and your time limited. If you are bored where you are, and feel able to get ahead, see your instructor and ask to go up to another class or group. He may well have spotted that you are doing well, and send you anyway, but it is your money and time that is being spent. If, on the other hand, you end up in a class that is too advanced, your instructor will quickly spot the fact (you'll fall down all the time), and send you somewhere more suitable. So, press on.

Ski-classes should be as small as possible, but inevitably seem to contain 12-20 people. Try and get into a small class. You will find the numbers shrink anyway as time goes on, but you will learn very little in a big class. Another advantage of going 'low season' is that the classes are smaller.

## SKI-ÉVOLUTIF

We are very much in favour of ski-évolutif.

The ski-évolutif or GLM (Graduated Length Method) as they call it in the USA, was pioneered in the French resort of Les Arcs in the 1960s. The technique is based on the beginner starting on short skis, of about 1 metre (39") in length, and doing advanced turns, parallels etc., right from the beginning. Such turns are much easier on a little ski. As the week passes, the same skills are practised, but on ever longer skis.

If ski-évolutif is on offer at your resort, take it. Try to learn ski-évolutif at your dry-ski classes, or artificial ski slope, before you go. If you are not going to learn by ski-évolutif, then dry or artificial ski on normal length skis. The aim should be to obtain continuity of technique and instruction, if possible.

## PRIVATE LESSONS

Private lessons are normally given before and after classes, and we are very much in favour of them once you have mastered the basic techniques. It is wasteful to have a private lesson on climbing a slope and the snow plough turn, but you might well consider them for stem christies, traversing, or side-slipping.

You don't have to have a private lesson on your own. Two or three of you at the same level can benefit greatly from a private lesson or two, with a competent instructor. Consider the time factor alone. In a class of say 12, doing stem turns, you might get to do your little bit, and receive some short advice ten times in two hours, after allowing for the hanging about and waiting and someone falling etc. In a private class of three, you ought, in one hour, to get twenty goes at a turn, and receive much more personal attention as well.

If you take this into account, then private lessons, if costly, are well worth the money. We found this particularly so with small children. Ours, aged 6, got very bored and cold standing in line. In a private lesson, they mopped up knowledge very swiftly, as children do at that age, and made excellent progress.

## STICK TO IT

For the absolute beginner, the first few days in the class lead to the crunch. You don't seem to be getting anywhere, and you're tired and you ache, and your feet hurt. By Wednesday, people are dropping out and swearing that ski-ing is just not for them. This is why, among other reasons, we recommend going for two weeks. It gives you time to have a day off, rest the feet, cheer up and start again. Have a private lesson if something defeats you.

Ski-ing is a sport, but it's a holiday too, and great fun. If you stick at it until you get off the nursery slope, you'll never regret it.

## Chapter 7

# STARTING TO SKI
# STANDING, WALKING, STOPPING, TURNING

To learn ski-ing properly you need competent instruction. However, even in the early days there are a few movements or turns
which, once mastered, make the whole business easier. Most of
the instruction in the next three chapters can be practised on your
own, on some moderate bump or slight slope near your hotel.
Practise these exercises because they will help you progress in
the classes.

## STANDING ON SKIS

The correct stance when on skis is most important. Too many
people look and feel very awkward when on skis, and from an
awkward beginning, a good turn or movement is barely possible.

Study the diagrams (Figure 19) carefully, and try and adopt the
position. On the flat, from the feet up, check as follows:

The skis should be slightly apart, and firmly on the ground, at
right angles to any slight slope on the ground. The ankles and
knees are flexed forward, but *from the knees to the shoulders the
body is erect but relaxed*. The weight rests firmly on both skis.

Read this again, and study the diagrams.

Look straight ahead. The arms are held slightly away from the
body, the hands just wider than the shoulders, about waist height.
Now relax. Don't flop, but don't be tense.

Re-read this passage again and assume this position a few
times, until you fall into it naturally.

Above all, try and avoid the "English lavatory position", with
legs straight and body bent forward from the hips. This position
is ungainly, unbalanced—and very common.

The above covers the correct ski stance for downhill running,
and standing on the flat. We will cover standing on the slopes
later.

## WALKING ON SKIS

With the feet in bindings, they cannot flex. To move you need to
slide the ski forward. Keep it flat on the snow, while reaching
forward with the opposite pole. Repeat, sliding the ski and bearing down on the pole. Pole and slide, pole and slide. As you begin
to gain momentum you can 'skate' a little on the skis, pushing off
the back foot, turning the front ski tip slightly outward, and

46

FIGURE 19

47

transferring all the weight onto it, just as if on skates. The first few times you will end up in a tangle, but it is worth persevering, for walking on the flat in skis, is a slow and effort-ful business. Off-piste and for any sort of distance it's better to take them off and carry them.

## CARRYING SKIS
The skis should be carried on the shoulder, tips forward and down. Clip them together with the rubber clip-straps. Carry the poles, for use as a walking stick.

## STOPPING
Even when on the flat, you may find that you have to stop quickly, or start to slide down some icy patch or slight incline. To stop, use the 'snow plough'. We will cover this in detail later but, in emergency:
1. Bend the knees in.
2. Turn the heels out.

Go 'knock-kneed'. This will bring the ski tips together, put the ends out, and 'edge' the ski. You will slither, probably somewhat awkwardly, to a stop.

Try not to stop by running into people, grabbing hold of posts or, even worse, fending yourself off with your pole-tip.

To stop before running out of piste, swing your arms and shoulders up the slope. This will transfer your weight, and you will turn up the slope and stop. Be careful you don't slide straight backwards, but, if you do, spread the ski tips out and edge them into the 'herringbone' position and you will stop.

## TURNING ON THE FLAT
People get in a terrible mess when trying to turn. Skis project out from your feet at the back and you stand on them and, Oh dear!— over you go. It's purely a beginner's problem. Once you get used to wearing skis, the problem disappears.

## STAR TURNS
These are used on the flat, or, with some 'edging', on moderate slopes.

Standing flat, and wanting to turn around, put one ski tip out to the side a bit, keeping the *tails of the skis together*. Now bring the other tip up to it, tails together. Now repeat and continue. You will be swivelling round like the hands on a clock, turning round backwards. To go round forward, the process is the same,

48

but you move the heels, keeping the tips together. If you get really good, you can go round heel and toe (Figure 20).

To start with, for the first two or three tries, don't move the tips too far apart, and keep the skis on or very close to the snow.

Slide, rather than lift the ski.

FIGURE 20

## KICK-TURNS

The kick-turn should only be used when in trouble, as for example, you are stuck on a steep slope, tips against the edge of the piste, and you are afraid of the fall-line. Unless you want to stay trans-fixed there for ever, you'll need to turn round and the kick-turn is the answer (Figure 21).

FIGURE 21

1. Turn the shoulders and look down the slope (eeeek!)
2. Place the downhill pole firmly in the snow by the end of the lower ski.
3. Place the uphill pole by the tip of the uphill ski.
4. Think about it. Put weight on uphill ski.
5. Lift the downhill ski clear of the snow, and turn the foot to place that ski parallel to the other, with the tip **outside** the lower pole.
6. Transfer weight to downhill ski.
7. Lift upper ski, turn the foot, and place below other ski. You have turned about.
8. Prepare to ski away.

Practise this on small but steep slopes, even on little bumps, but the steeper the slope the easier the turn.

You will find that the critical thing is the correct placing of the poles, one above and one below. Just get it right. Much weight rests on the arms, and you must remember to keep the knees as flexed as possible.

If you look like falling, fall backwards, to lie up the slope.

If, in fact, you get into a jam and are afraid to use the kick turn, and if the slope is not too long, then just fall over, uphill, lift skis clear of the snow, and roll around. It's pretty ungraceful and we wouldn't urge this course of action on you, but it is more important for the beginner to know how to overcome problems *somehow*, than to get panicky and lose confidence when confronted by them.

Always make your turn as early as possible, and try not to run out of piste.

## Chapter 8

## STARTING TO SKI
## CLIMBING, TRAVERSING AND SIDE SLIPPING

### THE FALL-LINE

The fall-line is the shortest, straightest line down any slope. If, to take a prosaic example, you were standing on a road bridge over a railway line, the white line painted down the middle of the road, on either side, would be running down the fall line. But a snow slope is covered in fall-lines. Because of bumps and the curve of the ground, you usually have to adjust yourself to a new fall-line every few metres. Fear of the fall-line is very common with beginners.

The fall-line is critical in ski-ing. Climbing up and ski-ing down is all done in relation to, or with reference to, the fall-line. So think about it and try not to worry about it.

### STANDING ON A SLOPE

If you are standing on a slope on your skis, both of them must be *ACROSS* the fall line.

If they are not, you will slide forward or back, or flounder around. If you find yourself doing these things then it is because you are not keeping your skis at right-angles to the fall line. Get them properly placed and you will feel more secure.

The upper ski should be slightly in front of the lower ski. Your weight rests on the lower ski, your hips and knees are turned into the slope, but you lean out. The steeper the slope, the more you lean out. It sounds, and looks unnatural, but it feels very safe.

### EDGING

If the slope is packed snow, crust, or icy, you will only be able to stand on it if you 'edge' your skis. You will 'edge' a lot in ski-ing, so just note here, that the most common error for beginners is to overdo the edging. 'Edge' just enough for your purpose and no more (Figure 22).

To stay on a slope, skis across the fall-line, turn the knees and and ankles *into the slope* until you seem to be resting on the edges *of the feet*. This will naturally turn the skis up, and let the slope-side 'edges' bite into the surface. If you try and turn the ski edges in, you are probably overdoing it, and straining the ankles.

The weight rests on the lower ski, the poles are turned into the

FIGURE 22

slope and placed behind you, and you lean out, away from the slope. Now relax.

## SIDE STEPPING (Figure 22)

From this position you can, by edging the skis into the slope, climb up it.

Face forward, arms and poles held as for a 'schuss'. Now, remembering to keep knees and ankles flexed into the slope, lift the weightless uphill ski and step sideways up the slope. 'Edge' it. Transfer your weight.

FIGURE 23

Bring up the lower ski, and so on. Keep the skis parallel and edged'. Don't plod, spring off the lower leg, but keep the steps short.

Climbing is fairly laborious, but if you transfer the weight neatly, and use mostly the leg muscles without heaving on your arms, you will not find it too taxing.

## HERRING-BONE CLIMB (Figure 23)

As you will have observed, side-stepping needs a bit of room, to accommodate the skis.

You may, however, have to climb a narrow path, up to the lift perhaps, where there is no room to turn sideways. In this situation use the herring-bone, so called from the pattern the climb imprints on the snow.

Face up the slope, and splay out the tips of your skis. Now bend the knees inwards (knock-kneed) and this will 'edge' the inside edge. The poles go behind you, and you lean the weight forward.

Now advance up the slope. You will need to keep the skis as wide apart as space permits, and to edge.

## TRAVERSING

Once you have climbed to the top of a slope you have to come down again.

You can, of course, run or 'schuss', straight down the fall line, but beginners usually shy away from this, at least to begin with. They come down by traversing, or crossing the slope at an angle, losing height, and using some sort of turn at the end of the slope.

A good starting position is essential to a neat traverse. See 'Standing on a Slope' (Figure 22).

Prepare to traverse by putting the skis across the fall-line, most weight on the lower ski, and look forward. Don't swivel the upper body down the slope. Keep it, and your gaze, in the direction you are going. The upper ski is slightly in front, arms relaxed, and slightly away from the body, knees and hips into the hill and lean out. The steeper the slope and the more icy the snow the more you will have to lean out and 'edge' the skis.

## RUNNING A TRAVERSE

From the position described above, all you have to do, is point the skis a little down the slope, give a push with the poles and off you go. Keep the knees flexed, the upper ski a little in front, look where you are going, and relax. If you go straight across the

FIGURE 24

slope you won't go very far or fast, but it is good practice (Figure 24).

However, beginners do make basic errors in traversing and if this could be eliminated easily then fewer bad habits would become engrained. Most of these errors come from fear of the fall-line.

Try, right from your first traverse, to point the tips down the slope, as much, and then a bit more, as your nerves permit.

It makes the traverse and the turn at the end easier. You have more speed, need not pole, and will slip across icy patches where slower ski-ers will fall.

So Rule One for traversing is to traverse as much *down* the slope as you can.

Rule Two comes in classes. The instructor will usually want you to follow in his tracks. You will feel that his line is much too steep, and you, with most of the class, will take a much more horizontal one.

Try not to. Hans or Mario has skied all his life. He is, by instinct and experience, taking the best traverse line for the slope. Follow his line and you will find the traverse and turn are easier. It may call for a little nerve initially, but you will find it easier.

Much of ski-ing is like that. A slope that appalls you on Monday, will bore you by Friday. You have mastered it. But you must first master yourself.

## SIDE-SLIPPING

In our opinion, the most useful manoeuvre the beginner can learn is the side-slip or skid. It forms a part of many turns, enables you to avoid trouble, helps you to lose height without turning, and is a graceful and enjoyable movement to perform. Therefore, although you may not be introduced to it for several days, we want to include it here.

To learn the basic side slip, seek out a large bump, the steeper the better; a 45° slope about ten or twelve feet high would be ideal.

Side-step up to the top. Then, standing 'well edged' on the top of the slope, face squarely down the slope, poles behind you, pole tips resting on the slope (Figure 25). Move the knees and ankles out, to flatten the ski on the slope, and slide down.

When you look back up the slope, having arrived at the bottom, you should see a broad, even, flattened track, marking your path.

FIGURE 25

There is a knack to this, rather like riding a bike, but do keep practising.

If you are with three or four other beginners, most of you will have the knack of side slipping inside half an hour. It gives a great sense of achievement. You will realise how useful a skill it is later, when traversng a slope, and realising that there is a rock in your path, or that the place you'd prefer to turn in is down there.

Flatten your skis as described, and you can slip below the obstacle or slide down to that nice smooth turning spot.

## DIAGONAL SIDE-SKID

Lean forward, towards the ski tips, when sliding, and you will skid forward as well as slide down. This manoeuvre is easier while moving in a traverse. Remember to maintain the traverse position, with the weight on the downhill ski. You really flatten the skis by rolling out the knees and ankles. Try this manoeuvre going round a bump, with a little speed on. That will be easier. Try and relax.

## SPEED

Ski-ing, like sailing, can give a quite erroneous impression of speed. You will see your class mates sliding quite slowly down a slope, shrieking (mostly with pleasure), and they will later assure you they were going like a rocket. You'll know different, but when it's your turn the sensation is the same. It's usually not more than about 20 mph., which over snow is perfectly safe. Provided you have control, speed is useful. Without some speed most movements are very difficult and quite exhausting.

## Chapter 9

## STARTING TO SKI
## SNOW-PLOUGHS, TURNING, FALLING, GETTING UP

In his first week, unless learning évolutif, the beginner will be taught the snow-plough turn. Later on he will rarely use it, although snow ploughing is a useful trick to know. The évolutif skier starts parallel turns at once, though cn very short skis, but the conventional skier learns the snow-plough as his first, basic turn.

### SNOW-PLOUGH TURN

To learn this, pick a long, fairly gentle slope. You need a long run, rather than a steep descent.

Get yourself in the snow-plough position (Figure 26) facing down the fall-line, and keep yourself there, with the poles in front. Now release yourself and you will, unless you are 'edging' too much, start to slide slowly down the slope. Keep the weight evenly on both skis. Do this two or three times until you are sliding easily, down the fall-line, in the snow-plough position.

Then, on the next go, bend the right knee, and transfer more weight slowly on to the right ski. You will find that this action turns your path to the left. If the turn continues up, like a fish-hook, you will stop.

Get organised on the fall-line, and descend again, but this time bend the left knee and transfer weight on to the left leg. You will turn to the right. Remember, and note, that you are leaning *out* of the turn.

Continue practising until you can turn to either side evenly. Examine the tracks after each turn and check for deep grooves. These indicate excessive 'edging'. Try and keep the skis flat.

### LINKED PLOUGH TURNS

Now go back to the top of your long slope. Get in the snow-plough position, facing down the fall-line, and descend, but this time try and link the turns. Descend like the letter 'S', not turning up like a fish-hook. Keep the skis flat, and turn by transferring the weight smoothly and gently from one side to the other.

At the bottom, stop, using the 'edges', in the snow-plough position. Side-step up the slope, and carry on practising.

FIGURE 26

An afternoon like this, practising the snow-plough turn, the side slip and the traverse, will help your progress in class tremendously, and get you fit at the same time.

## FALLING DOWN AND GETTING UP

Everybody falls. Don't let it depress you. The falling is easy, it's the getting up time after time that wears you out.

Since you don't usually want to fall, giving guidance on how to do so may seem superfluous, but quite often you will know that you are going to fall, and have some little choice of where and how.

Try and fall up the slope. If the slope is steep, you have less distance to fall, your skis are below to act as brakes, and you are ready to rise again. If you fall head-first down the slope, you may carry on sliding. You will have fallen over the top of your skis which is risky, and a lot of floundering around is inevitable. Don't fall back on to the skis, or they will keep going with you lying on the back. Try and fall in a compact position, elbows in, head down, legs together. You can break arms and collar bones as well as ankles, so fall neatly. *ONCE DOWN* you may end up in a terrible tangle—skis crossed, one dug deep, one out of the binding, ski poles trapped beneath you. You may need help, especially in deep, heavy snow.

First advice though, is to lie still a minute, get your breath, and decide if you have broken every bone in your body. When you discover you haven't, try and roll on to your back, and get the legs in the air. This should lift the skis clear of the snow and you can lie flat and start to get organised. Remove your hands from the pole-loops, but be sure the poles don't slip or roll away.

Clean any snow off boots and bindings, replace the boots on the skis, if necessary, and prepare to stand up. Get the skis across the fall-line. Grasp the two poles together, one hand by the baskets, the other at the straps. Lie on your side. Draw up the legs, and get the weight forward. Now, leaning one hand on the pole baskets and pulling up on the other, heave yourself upright. Use the leg muscles rather than the arms.

Dust off any excess snow, replace glasses or goggles, and away you go.

## Chapter 10

## SAFETY, SKI-ING RULES AND PRECAUTIONS

In all Venture Guides we lay stress on safety. In ski-ing, as in most sports, there are a few rules, which if followed by the individual, make things more enjoyable and safer for everyone.

Please note and observe the following:

1. Don't fool about on lifts or tows. Don't push in the queue.
2. If you fall, on piste or tow track, get out of the way, fast, before you start to get up.
3. Don't let the tow bar fly off, as someone may be in the way.
4. If you are overtaking another ski-er, it is your responsibility to keep clear. He may turn suddenly, remember, but it is the overtaking ski-er's responsibility to avoid those in front, in all circumstances.
5. Don't start off without a good look around.
6. Never ski fast over a crest. Know what's on the other side, or stop and look.
7. On a traverse, overtake *above* the front ski-er. Then he can't turn down into you.
8. Don't stop in the middle of the piste.
9. Don't walk on the piste in ski boots—it makes holes in the snow where others can catch a tip.
10. Never ski off-piste on your own.
11. Ski under control. If you lose control stop. If you *can't* stop— try a controlled fall. Don't hurtle on until stopped by a tree or a crowd of beginners.
12. Obey any danger or diversion signals. Never ski a barred route or on an 'avalanche' slope. Ski-ers are killed every year because they ignore these signs.

As you can see, these all boil down to common sense and good manners, but common sense is somewhat uncommon, and good manners are becoming rare.

## INSURANCE AND SOCIAL SECURITY

Always go adequately insured. Insure yourself not just for medical treatment but for transportation and time off work. Remember that if you get injured, medical costs in Europe have to be paid for at a much higher rate than at home. So be sure your cover is adequate. You don't have to break a leg to need medical attention.

Incidentally, provided you are fit and obey the rules, get the muscles warm before you start a descent and don't bite off more

63

than you can chew, ski-ing is a perfectly safe pursuit. We have been ski-ing for twenty years and have suffered no more than some bad bruising—(Yet! touch wood!).


## ACCIDENTS

Accidents do happen. If you see someone take a bad fall and not get up, ski over and see what's up.

If the injured ski-er doesn't speak your language beckon other ski-ers over until you find one who can talk to the injured party. There are usually ski patrols out on the main slopes, or someone will alert the ambulance sled which is usually kept at the top of the main lift. Ask someone to go down and advise the lower lift attendant, just in case no-one has yet done so.

Meanwhile, don't pick the casualty up. Remove his skis gently, and stick them in the snow, crossed, like an 'X'. This will quickly indicate the site of the accident to the descending 'blood waggon'. Keep the casualty as warm as you can, and give some reassurance.

Stay with him. Ideally, except that you cannot know the extent of the injuries, he should be placed in the 'recovery position', supported on his side with the cheek resting on the ground, for, after a severe fall, in fright and pain, a casualty may vomit. People die after simple accidents, choking on their own vomit, when lying on their backs, so stay with the casualty, and if he is sick, help him to clear his mouth. It's unpleasant, but it may save a life. A good knowledge of First Aid is useful to all outdoor enthusiasts, ski-ers not excepted.


## PRECAUTIONS

Prevention, as they say, is better than cure, so a few precautions may keep you out of trouble. Be sure you are warm enough, and stop before you get over-tired. Remember a five mile trip out means a five mile trip back—that makes ten miles, and are you up to it? Take some chocolate to keep the energy up.

Get fit, or at least fitter. At the top of every lift, warm your leg muscles before the descent. Side-step up a little slope, or stamp around a bit. Wear gloves. Check your bindings, edges and equipment in general, frequently. If something looks loose or frayed, have it seen to. Finally, use your common sense.

## ICE AND 'WHITE OUTS'

You can run into ice suddenly on a shaded slope, under trees, early in the morning, and when the clouds come down. So use your eyes and watch out for it. Use your ears too. The first sign is usually a sudden rasping sound from your skis. The answer is to use lots of 'edge', and, therefore, be sure your edges are sharp, as smooth edges will slip on ice.

A 'White Out' occurs when the clouds come down. It is simply a fog, but what with the white snow, and the mist, all shape is gone, and you find yourself ski-ing in a void.

Stay with your group, and stay on the piste. If you are on your own, stop and listen. You may hear the sound of other ski-ers, or the sound of the lifts, which usually keep running. Ski slowly, losing height, in the direction of the sound. 'White Outs' happen quite frequently and are no cause for alarm, but a degree of caution is advisable. Following the lifts down, until the piste crosses the track is a useful hint.

If you are on the piste, and want to stop, go to the side. The big risk then is from madmen bombing down the piste in poor visibility. On the way down follow the piste markers.

If you are really lost and bewildered in a White Out, stop, wait, and shout for help (just shout HELP!).

# Part 2

# Cross Country Skiing

## Chapter 1

# WHAT IS CROSS COUNTRY SKI-ING?

Historically, cross-country ski-ing is the original form of the sport, dating back probably to prehistoric times.

Certainly there are cave paintings from the Neolithic period, around 30,000BC which appear to show people on skis. Alpine ski-ing, on the other hand, is barely a hundred years old, although in that time it has come to dominate the sport, and even oust cross-country or Nordic ski-ing from dominance in its traditional areas.

Perhaps before we go any further, we had better clear up the problem of the name. Cross-country ski-ing, as we have noted, has a variety of names, with practically every country, and certainly every language having its own. We use the term 'cross country ski-ing' as the name for the sport in this book because it is the most descriptive, both of the sport itself, and of those areas we will cover in this book. We will refer to it as 'ski-ing' and refer to Alpine ski-ing as "downhill" ski-ing.

## A DEFINITION

Cross country ski-touring is the process of moving on skis, over snow-covered terrain, off the downhill 'piste', either through deep untrodden snow, or on prepared cross-country tracks. It employs equipment which differs in many ways from downhill equipment which is used on different terrain, and requires a number of different and supporting skills.

Exactly what these skills and differences are we shall cover in subsequent chapters.

## WHY CROSS COUNTRY?

It is reasonable to enquire into this current renaissance of cross country ski-ing, for it is booming away in many countries, but the reasons are not hard to seek.

First of all, given snow cover of a few inches, you can XC-ski anywhere, so that it opens up vast areas unsuited to the downhill ski-er.

## COST

Secondly, compared with downhill, cross-country is cheap. A complete and adequate set of skis, boots, poles and bindings, can be bought for less than $100 dollars, although

**Fig. 1**

you can pay much more if you want to. You don't need lifts, which, with Alpine lift passes reaching about $50 a week is a great saving, and you can avoid the crowds on the slopes and congestion on the lifts.

## CLOTHING

While you *can* buy attractive and colourful XC garments, you can get along very well in just warm and comfortable old clothes, which is another saving. (Fig. 2)

## IS IT DULL?

No, it isn't.

If you have been a downhill ski-er, with the occasional lift-borne tour thrown in, you will probably find, when you try cross-country, that this is the sort of ski-ing you wanted when you took up the sport. On cross-country skis you can get away from the crowds, and get that exhilaration and sense of freedom that can no longer be found on crowded 'pistes'.

XC requires a good standard of ski-ing and while you usually climb up, there is always the downhill swoop to follow, through the deep, unmarked snow, to give you a thrill and test your skills.

## AGE

Age is no barrier to cross-country. You can start very young, and go on for ever. It is less dangerous to limbs than downhill, and gives more physical satisfaction. Given a steady start, and good technique you will not find it too exhausting. You don't need to be super-fit, (although it helps) but cross-country will get and keep you fit. Cross-country will appeal to those who like the outdoors for itself, to walkers, hikers, campers and ramblers — as well as ski-ers. If you want to get about in the winter, do it on cross-country skis.

## WHERE CAN YOU GO XC?

Almost anywhere, is the short answer. All you need is snow, Traditionally, cross-country has been firmly based in the Scandinavian countries, Norway, Sweden, Finland, and it still is. Their equipment and techniques set the standard for the world. But the sport has spread widely. Canada and the U.S.A. have huge cross-country areas, Australia and New Zealand are experiencing a boom, while in France the Pyrenees, the Auvergne, and the Vosges, all specialize in cross-country, and XC is now seen, a little more each year, in the committed Alpine ski resorts.

It is still difficult, outside Scandinavia and North America, to find holidays devoted to·cross-country ski-ing, but this will undoubtedly come. Meanwhile, it certainly exists at more and more downhill resorts, and you can sample it under private arrangements when you get there.

Chapter 2

## CLOTHING

It is fair to say that, initially anyway, any old sports clothes will do. However, a wide range of attractive and suitable gear exists, at reasonable prices, and it may be comforting to look the part even if, to begin with, you can't manage the technique. (Fig. 2)

## BODY HEAT AND VENTILATION

Even though you are out in the snow, at below or near zero temperatures, you will not be cold if you keep moving. The exercise will keep you warm, but it is important to keep as cool and as free from perspiration as possible. If your clothing gets damp from sweat, it loses most of the insulation properties, and you will chill rapidly when you stop unless you then put on windproof garments to keep the wind out until your body cools.

Bear in mind that the real chill comes from cooling perspiration, not from the effect of the cold air. Your garments, therefore, must be lightweight and of a natural material, equipped with buttons or zips to aid ventilation while moving, but enabling you to cover up quickly and retain warmth when you stop.

Cross-country ski-ing is warm work, so for a normal day's outing the clothes tend to be lightweight, and must allow free movement.

Leaving aside the boots, which will be covered in the next chapter, let us start at the feet and work up.

## STOCKINGS

You need to wear two pairs. One long pair, knee-length, and preferably of oiled wool, and a short pair, of just over ankle length, to go on top of the first long pair. The idea is that you fold the top of the short pair over the boot, to make a better seal against the snow. Personally, I think gaiters do a neater and better job, so I wear gaiters as well.

## KNICKERS

Knickers, (or breeches, as they call them in England ) are the ideal lower garment for the cross-country ski-er. I have a pair of lightweight knickers in a tough tweed-mix. They fasten, below the knee, over the stockings, with Velcro strips, have button through pockets and a double seat. I use them for hill walking and

73

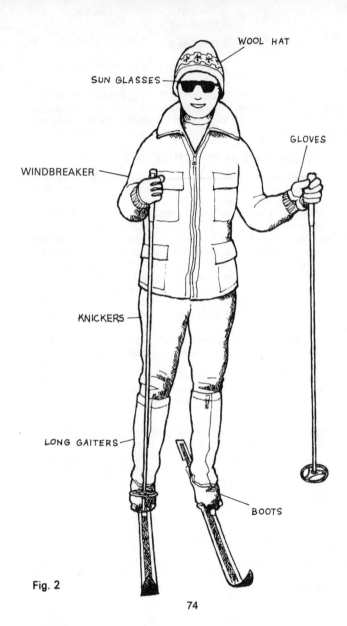

WOOL HAT

SUN GLASSES

GLOVES

WINDBREAKER

KNICKERS

LONG GAITERS

BOOTS

Fig. 2

74

scrambling in the summer, and for cross-country work in winter. Ordinary outdoor trousers or stretch ski-pants can be temporarily transformed into breeches by simply rolling long stockings up over them to the knee.

## SWEATSHIRTS

A light T-shirt, not too tight under the arms, is ideal. Any old wool or cotton shirt will do. This soaks up the sweat, and retains some insulation properties when you stop.

## ANORAK/PARKA

Over the top goes a light single-skin anorak in proofed nylon. It has a full length zip, as it is usually open when on the move. Zipped and flapped pockets keep the wet out and the flaps prevent the zips from freezing. It is a good idea to have a hood, which can be rolled back into the collar, until needed.

## HAT

Many cross-country ski-ers favour a peaked hat, which keeps twigs out of your eyes when dodging under trees.

One of these, or a wool hat which can be pulled over the ears is fine. I also carry an ear-band, which is very handy in the warm days. Hats soak up sweat from the head and forehead, and when ski-ers stop for a snack or chat it's not unusual to see the sweat freezing up on their hat bands!

## GLOVES

Gloves get pretty wet, so a good pair which retain their insulation when damp via an absorbent lining is a worthwhile buy. Strong leather palms and fingers, matched with a breathable meshed top would be fine. Buy a pair big enough to get a cotton pair on as well, to keep you warm in bad weather. Some folk swear by mittens, but since they are always having to come off —to open the pack or fiddle with the compass, I prefer gloves.

## SKI-SUITS

As cross-country ski-ing grows in popularity, a whole wardrobe of lightweight, attractive clothing is coming on to the market. They are usually made of light cotton, or breathable nylon, in striking colours, and are very glamorous. They are available in two-part outfits, or as a complete overall.

## UNDERWEAR

Unless it is very cold, excessive underwear will simply lead to overheating. A light cotton singlet and pants would probably be best.

## SPARE CLOTHING

The above selection will look after you adequately on the move, but it is as well to have some extras, and something to carry them in.

## GAITERS

If you wear knee-length gaiters you will have gone a long way towards keeping snow out of your boots, and preventing it from chilling your feet. Even when travelling on prepared tracks, a pair of ankle gaiters or "Stop-Tous" are useful. Long gaiters also come in handy at lunch time, for you can sit on one, insulating the rear, and spread out your lunch on the other. Buy a pair of gaiters as a *basic* item.

## SPARE SWEATER/DUVET

A thick wool sweater or a 'duvet' or fibre pile jacket is a useful item for when you stop. Neither need weigh very much, and if rolled up small and tucked into the bottom of the rucksack, they are out of the way and yet to hand if you need them.

## SPARE SOCKS

These are always useful. Why be miserable if you can avoid it? In very cold conditions wet feet can be dangerous, so while I would not advise you, in normal conditions, to change the socks the minute you step in a stream (for you might shortly step in another one), if your feet are wet and getting chilled, then change your socks.

## SUN GLASSES — GOGGLES

Always have a pair of each.

There is a whole list of bits and pieces, waxes etc., which we shall look at later (see chapter 4) but for them, as for the clothes, you need a rucksack.

Fig. 3

Chapter 3

# BOOTS, BINDINGS, POLES, SKIS

Cross-country equipment is light. The work it does is hard. It follows therefore, that the equipment must be strong and designed by experts for the job it has to do. It is now much more sophisticated than it was even five years ago, and no doubt variety and innovations will continue to appear.

Do not skimp on equipment, but buy the best you can afford. Fortunately cross-country gear is relatively cheap and if you look after it, it will last for years. Now let's go through the equipment item by item, noting the points to look out for when buying.

## BOOTS

At present, and for the foreseeable future, the best boots come from Norway. Insist on Norwegian or at least Scandinavian boots, and you will be on the right track. Above all, the boots *must* fit well. Most boots are now produced to the *Nordic Norm,* which ensures that any boot will fit any binding. (Fig. 3)

When going to buy boots, take with you, or borrow from the shop, the normal two pairs of socks, one thick long pair, and a short, thinner pair.

A cross-country boot looks rather like a running shoe, but if you examine it carefully it has, or should have, some special features. Different types of ski-touring, racing, or mountaineering require different types of boots. Let's look here at touring boots.

The sole at the toe projects into a wide extended flap. On the underside at this point, three holes are drilled into the sole. These are to take the pins on the binding, and it is better if each hole is fitted with a brass sleeve, which stops the holes from becoming ragged or filling in with grit.

Flex the sole. The heel should bend up with supple ease but there should be no sideways movement. Try and twist the instep. It should be impossible, for the instep should be reinforced with a steel or wood insert, to give rigidity against any lateral play. Without this your foot will slip off the ski in the turns.

The boot is single-skinned, usually lined with fur, light and (thank goodness) comfortable. There should be no question of 'breaking in' a cross-country boot — if it isn't comfortable in the shop, try another pair. The types illustrated (Fig. 3) are right for normal cross-country and touring. Heavier boots are needed for ski-mountaineering.

Notice that the boot is single skinned. It will let in the wet, and for this reason you need two pairs of socks, and you should also treat the boot with some water-repellent preparation. The snag is that if it is truly water repellent, it prevents the foot from breathing, and perspiration gets the foot wet anyway. A sensible compromise is to keep the boots clean and well polished, which will help make them waterproof, or use Kiwi wet-prufe.

## BINDINGS

As with boots, the choice of binding depends on the type of XC ski-ing you want. For general or light touring the most common and successful binding currently in use is the three-pin Nordic type by Rotefella or Troll. In these, three metal pins in the front of the binding fit into the holes in the boot sole. The binding clamp is then forced down over a spring ratchet, and the toe is clamped securely to the ski. These are also produced to the "Nordic Norm" in standard widths of 71 mm. 75 mm. and 79 mm. The 75 mm. is the most popular. (Fig. 4)

Although the heel can rise, there is also a serrated metal or plastic 'popper' or heel plate, which is situated on the ski, directly under the heel. This will grip the boot heel when your weight is down, for turning or stopping.

Most bindings are a standard 75 mm. size, which will fit most boots. If your feet are very large or very small, you may need to order a special binding. Note that there is a left and right binding and they are usually so marked.

## CABLES

Many downhill ski-ers taking up XC, worry about the lack of a cable or clamp securing the boot heel down, when descending, turning or stopping. Given the right technique, practice, and a heel plate, a clamp cable is not necessary and, if fitted to a Nordic binding, positively dangerous. The cable will force the boot into the binding and should you fall, the binding will not release, as a downhill safety binding (usually) does. A broken ski or ankle is the possible outcome. Cable bindings are used by ski-mountaineers where the binding can be adjusted up for climbing, and yet still clamp the heel down for descent. A 'release' safety feature is essential.

There *are* safety bindings for ski-mountaineering, but for normal cross country work they are not necessary, although in some countries cables are a standard fitting.

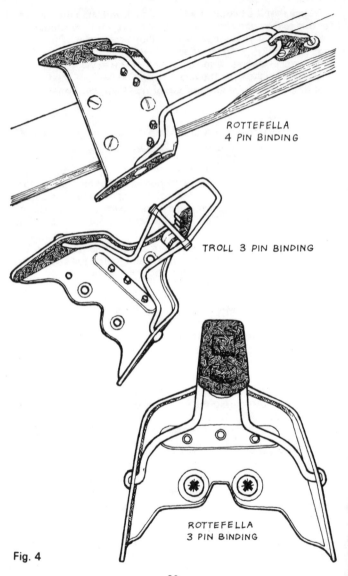

ROTTEFELLA
4 PIN BINDING

TROLL 3 PIN BINDING

ROTTEFELLA
3 PIN BINDING

Fig. 4

## POLES

Until quite recently all cross-country poles were of Tonkin bamboo. Bamboo poles are still available, inexpensive and very popular. However, having nearly impaled myself when a bamboo pole splintered under me, I have purchased, at moderate cost, an aluminium pair, and I recommend you to do likewise. Fibreglass poles are coming on to the market and they are said to be excellent.

Cross-country poles are long. To be the right length they should fit comfortably into the armpit, like crutches. They would be light in weight, yet strong enough to support your weight while you cross a fence or obstacle.

The straps should be adjustable, and worn under the palms and over the back of the wrist. Note the drawing of the basket and ferrule (Fig. 5). The ferrule tip is slanted forward to ease its exit from the snow as you glide through. The baskets are usually of plastic, and fairly large for greater support off the track or in deep snow. The holes are wide to let the snow slip off easily.

## SKIS

Even more than with the downhill variety, you could have a whole book on cross-country skis alone. (Fig. 5)

We have already defined the sort of ski-ing we intend to do, which narrows the choice somewhat. The next decision has more crucial long term effects.

## WHICH TYPE OF SKI?

It depends (again) on the type of ski-ing you want. Decide:—
1. If you enjoy backpacking and winter camping.
2. Do you prefer prepared trails, or off-piste deep snow?
3. Do you want to race or tour?
4. Which sort of terrain will you commonly ski over? Downland, hills, woods, fells, mountains?
5. What is your standard of fitness and XC skill?

## WAX OR NON-WAX

Until recently, all cross-country skis were made of wood, and all wood needs waxing. Then along came synthetic skis, in came fibreglass, plastic, or polyethylene, which still need waxing but with less preparation. Now there are skis with so-called non-wax surfaces, and, if you buy these your waxing problems are considerably reduced. BUT . . . and there is always a *'but'*, it is undisputed (at present) that waxed skis perform better than the non-waxed.

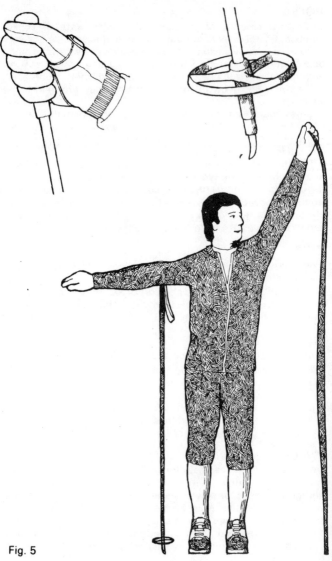

Fig. 5

It is therefore likely that if you start cross-country ski-ing and like it you will want to do better, which means waxing. And then what do you do with your step-cut non-wax skis? Let us lay out the broad pros and cons for each type and you can decide for yourself.

There are basically three sorts of cross country ski-ing, and three sorts of skis, differentiated by weight and width.

## RACING SKIS
These are very light, around 3 lbs (1.5 kilos), the pair, and made of fibreglass. They are narrow, less than 50 mm (2") wide at the binding, and naturally quite fragile. They are too delicate for general cross-country work, and until you start racing or want to go in for high speed travel, they are not for you.

## LIGHT TOURING SKIS
These vary between 52 and 56 mm in width at the binding, and weigh around 4-5 lbs (3 kilos) the pair, and are the best ski for the good ski-er, especially if the bulk of the ski-ing is on prepared trails.

## GENERAL TOURING SKIS
If you want to concentrate on climbing hills, or bashing through the woods off prepared trails, then these are the skis for you. They are fairly wide, 56-60 mm (2.25"). As they are wider they give better support in really deep soft snow, and as they are heavier and stiffer some beginners find them easier to manage. However, once you have picked up the technique, they can feel a little cumbersome, weighing anything from 5 to 7 lbs. (3 kilos) the pair, and you may then prefer the light-touring ski.

## WHICH SORT OF SKI-ING?
As you can see, the choice of equipment is governed by the type of cross-country ski-ing you have in mind. In this book we are assuming that one starts the sport by touring on tracks or across moderate country. For this the light touring ski is the best but the general touring ski is easier for the beginner. We shall concentrate on describing the general type in this book, and ignore the heavier steel edged ski-mountaineering ski completely.

## SKI-ING SURFACES
The cross-country ski market is in a state of expansion and continual change. New techniques and materials are being introduced all the time. In every case the trend is towards finding a way to avoid waxing, or at least reduce it to running waxes. Let

me briefly explain that there are, **basically** two sorts of waxes. "Running" waxes give you grip while you 'kick', yet permit you to slide. **"Base"** waxes hold the running wax to the ski, or base preparation necessary with wooden skis. Running waxes go in the middle of the ski and 'gliding' waxes, a variation, if used at all, go at the end(s). We will cover all this in more detail later.

Please bear with us throughout, on the thorny subject of names. The same items are called different things by different authorities, and vary from country to country.

We try here to **either** define any name or reference, **or** use the most self-explanatory phrase.

## SKI TYPES

Broadly speaking, skis come in four basic materials:

1. *Wood:* the best wood skis are made from birch, or hickory, are usually laminated, and edged with lignostone, a hardwood formed from compressed beech. With a wooden ski, the full wax treatment is required, which consists of tarring, preparing with base waxes, then waxing, corking down the running waxes etc. Treated wood holds wax well, and the skis look very beautiful. I fancy, though, that they will slowly disappear or become very costly. It is, of course, possible to get a wood ski with a plastic or fibreglass bottom.

2. *Synthetic Surfaces:* More and more fibreglass, or plastic-soled skis are being produced. They are hard-wearing, and although they don't take wax as well as wood, they need much less preparation. This is particularly true of those fibreglass skis with a plastic bottom. Some models have a numbered waxing scale on the ski sole which lets you know or judge just how large an area you have waxed, which is a useful feature. These need base waxes and running waxes.

3. *Non-wax Step-cut:* The non-wax ski is the latest development. Many such skis now have indentations cut in the sole making a step or fishscale pattern, stretching for about a metre under the foot. The idea is that these patterns grip the snow when you are 'kicking' and yet permit a smooth 'glide' when you move. The makers claim they grip well and need no waxing, which, up to a point, is true. They work very well in 'Klister' conditions (Page 93) but are less effective in powder snow or on ice, make a considerable noise, and in my opinion, need some paraffin glide wax to reduce drag. The pattern can wear out after a while.

84

4. *Mohair Strips:* This is a variation on the step-cut idea, and is designed to eliminate the need for 'kicking' waxes. Thin mohair strips are let into the base of the ski and they do provide a good grip. They wear well and are easily replaced. I find they are a little less effective in providing a clean glide, but they work very well in temperatures 10°F either side of freezing. They are *very* good in "Klister" conditions. No doubt new types of ski will soon appear.

## HOW MUCH SKI-ING
To decide which sort to buy you have to guess how much ski-ing you are going to do. It is safe to suggest fibreglass over wood, but then it depends how much opportunity you are going to get to actually ski, although remember that, providing you've got the snow, you can cross-country ski almost anywhere — the local park, along a footpath, even round the garden. However, if you are an occasional weekend or holiday ski-er, then I would recommend a mohair or step-cut non-wax ski. Waxing is a technique where the ability grows with experience. If you only ski occasionally you will learn little and forget a lot, so a non-wax ski might be less trouble. However, you should still learn about waxes, for even step-cut skis work better with it.

## FITTING SKIS
Let us now consider the features you should look for when buying or hiring skis.

## LENGTH
Cross-country skis are long. The best guide is to hold the hand up over your head, and choose the ski where the tip fits comfortably into the palm of the upheld hand. Beginners hiring skis might prefer skis a little shorter, say with the tip reaching just to the upheld wrist, while if you are tall or heavy, then perhaps one a little longer would be better. (Fig. 5)

## CAMBER AND FLEXIBILITY
Cross-country skis, held base to base, exhibit a considerable curve or "camber". Grasp the skis between fingers and thumb in the high arch, and squeeze them together. Check that they lie flat together all along their length, as any failure to do so indicates distortion.

Camber is the amount of arc or curve in the skis. The amount of resistance to flattening is called 'flex'. Your weight must be spread evenly along the entire length, and it is the 'camber' that does this, and thereby assists the 'kick' and 'glide' phases.

The skis should come together firmly, but without undue difficulty. If they snap together the skis are too soft, too flexible,

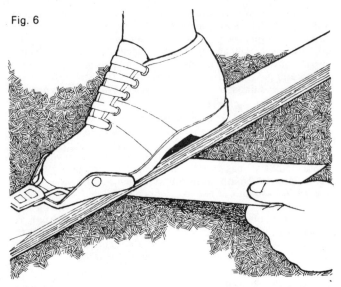

Fig. 6

and the tips and tails may rise when your weight goes on them. If they are virtually impossible to squeeze together, they are too stiff, and you may not rest evenly on the snow. So you want skis that you can squeeze together with some little effort.

Try another test. Lay the skis down on a hard even floor (not a carpet) and stand on them. Have the assistant try to slip a piece of paper under them, at the point below your feet. The sheet of paper should slide under easily. If it won't, the skis are too soft for your weight. If, on the other hand you can get a wedge of cardboard under, they are too stiff. (Fig. 6)

Don't neglect these tests.

Let us now summarise. Remember that you do not have to buy, for you can usually hire, even in downhill resorts nowadays and in the beginning, until you are certain that you like cross-country ski-ing, and have decided what sort, and how much you will be able to do, hiring is far the best.

If you buy, we recommend general touring equipment throughout, with fibreglass skis, rather than wood, and that you give serious consideration to a non-wax type, while remembering that they are relatively untried, and less effective. Think it over, talk to the sales assistant, and while you are at it, invest in a few bits and pieces.

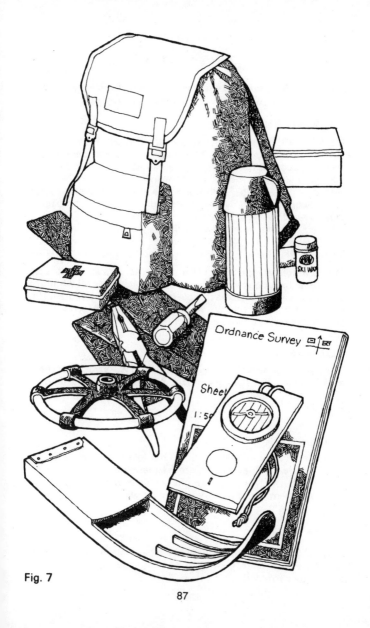

Fig. 7

87

## Chapter 4

# ACCESSORIES

For ski-touring, you need a few items which, if you are a summer hiker or camper, you may well possess anyway. (Fig. 7)

## TOURING RUCKSACK

A small, light, frameless, nylon rucksack is a useful buy. Karrimor have an excellent selection, and the sort suitable for day hiking is also very suitable for cross-country ski-ing. Try it on and be sure that it fits snugly to the back. Any swaying about will upset your balance while ski-ing. For the same reason a waist belt is useful. Some people use a downhill ski-ers bumbag, but I don't believe these are adequate for cross-country work.

Here are a few items to put in it.

## SPARE SKI TIP

This is a hollow replica, in metal or plastic, of a ski tip. It is not difficult to break a ski in the woods and if it shears off when you are in the wilds you'll have trouble getting home. The spare tip fits on to the body of the ski, is secured there with screws or a serrated clamp, and will get you home.

## COMPASS

Even on a short outing take a compass, and work out beforehand the bearings to the road or car park. A route card for your day tour is a sensible preparation.

## MAP

You need a local map(s) of a scale not less than 1:50,000, and given that winter landmarks are frequently obscured, 1:25000 might be better. Neither map nor compass will help you if you can't use them and if you are unfamiliar with map and compass.

## FIRST AID KIT

A small kit containing bandages, a few plasters, 'Moleskin' for blisters, and some face and sun cream for chapped face and lips, should be carried.

## POLE BASKET

It's quite easy also to wrench the basket off the pole, having caught it under some tree root. Ski-ing without a basket is a lopsided affair, so buy a spare, complete with split-pin, and put it in the sack. A plastic or bamboo one weighs next to nothing, and is easily stowed.

## SKI-BAG

When you buy your skis buy a bag to carry them in. This is particularly important if you intend transporting the skis by car, in a ski or roof rack. Rain, spray and flying grit harm the skis, and wax won't stick to wet or dirty surfaces. So buy a ski bag.

## REPAIR OUTFIT

A small screwdriver and a pair of needle-point pliers are useful.

## VACUUM FLASK — FOOD PACK

A meal out, even a picnic lunch, is a great part of the day, and in winter a warm drink is welcome. Prepare it beforehand and take it in a vacuum flask, padding the flask with your extra sweater. Consider taking cold drinks as well. Cross-country ski-ing is thirsty work and you can get dehydrated.

## LUNCH BOX

A plastic lunch box, or a Tupperware container is ideal, and weighs very little.

Finally, you will need a wax kit, containing a range of waxes, suitable for your area, and so, let us now look at waxes and waxing.

Chapter 5

# WAXES AND WAXING

Nothing so preoccupies the cross country ski-er as waxes and waxing. The subject offers endless opportunities for discussion, argument, expertise and error. To the experienced ski-er all this is great fun, but to the beginner it is confusing and a little worrying. Let us start by assuring the beginner that there is very little to worry about. A few simple rules and guidelines will quickly overcome most of the problems you may encounter.

How much time you spend waxing depends on your skis, which fall into three main types.

1. *Wooden skis:* Wooden skis need the full waxing treatment. The raw wood base must be sealed with tar against wet. This is followed by a base wax, which serves as a 'base' for the full range of running waxes. Tars can be melted on , painted on or come in spray-cans.

2. *Skis with synthetic running surfaces:* Most racing skis, even wooden ones now have synthetic bottoms, of glass or carbon fibre. These need base waxes *and* running waxes.

3. *Non-Wax Skis:* No waxing required; but I have a step-cut pair, and while they are fine for climbing and very effective on the flat, I find them slow downhill, and use a little glide wax on tips and tails.

Waxes come in two basic categories: base waxes (sometimes called sealer-waxes), and running waxes (sometimes called kicking, climbing or glide waxes). Running waxes are broadly broken down into hard waxes, and 'klisters'. A first point is that the colder and newer the snow, the harder the wax. Klisters are for old, soft snow, and in "above zero" temperatures.

## BASIC WAXING RULES

If you follow the following rules most of your problems will be little ones.

1. Stick to one manufacturer's brand of wax.
2. Read the instructions on can or tube before applying.
3. Remember a soft wax gives more grip than a hard wax, but less glide.
4. Remember that you can put a soft wax on a hard wax but not vice-versa.
5. Wax neatly, making a good job improves the result.
6. Several *thin* layers give more grip than one *thick* one.

7. If you have too much 'grip' try rubbing the wax out thinner with a cork.
8. Remember that freezing point is 0°C or 32°F. Above 0°C the snow is wet — below 0°C the snow is dry.
9. Learn to judge the snow by feel (Page 96).
10. Apply the wax to dry skis — it won't go on otherwise.

Now, since that seems a lot of rules, let's just go into the reasoning.

1. Most manufacturers code waxes by colour, but use a different range of colours. Stick to one brand and you'll know where you are.
2. For the same reason read the instructions, one man's 'klister' is another man's poison! Waxes come in cans, klister in tubes.
3. & 4. If you put a hard wax on top of a soft wax it will just cut through — because it's harder! You will have to scrape the soft wax off to apply a hard wax — so if in doubt use a harder wax first.
5, 6 & 7. A neat job gives better results. Read the application instructions and 'cork' the job properly if required. A good corking improves a good waxing, and you can often thin out the wax by rubbing it down with a cork and get more glide, without scraping the lot off and starting again.
8 & 9. The basic decision is between wet and dry snow, but the permutations are endless. See waxing chart (page 96).
10. That's why we told you to buy a ski bag for transportation. You are better off waxing indoors, but the skis must be put outside to adjust to the temperature before you start to ski.

## WAXING KIT

The basic kit consists of just three items:

1. Some waxes and klisters (Page 93).
2. A waxing cork.
3. A scraper.

Buy a plastic bag to put them in, as loose waxes can make a mess. As time goes on and you get more experienced you will also want:—

4. Solvents (for cleaning the wax off),
5. A waxing iron — for melting and spreading wax on skis.
6. A waxing torch; a mini-blowtorch for putting on base wax, removing old wax, and warming the waxing iron.

Fig. 8

## WAXES AND KLISTERS

Each major manufacturer supplies about a dozen running waxes and klisters, plus a range of base preparations, compounds and cleaners.

'Running waxes' fall into two groups:

**Hard Waxes:** These come in little colour coded cans, and are, broadly speaking used for new dry snow, and powder.

**Klisters:** 'Klister' is a Norwegian word, meaning 'sticky', and klisters are sticky waxes that come in colour-coded tubes or sometimes in aerosol cans. Klister is used for older, slushy, or settled packed snow. It gives grip.

*To this basic range we have to add:*

**Glide Waxes:** These are often paraffin based, and go on plastic or fibreglass bottoms — even on the tips and tails of non-wax skis — to increase *glide.*

**Base Waxes** (sealers): These are used to help running waxes adhere to the ski, and are used on synthetic skis and the wood-soled variety.

**Base Preparations** (Tars): These are not waxes at all. Tars are used to seal wooden skis against damp, and provide a base for the base waxes.

## HOW TO WAX

If you have wooden skis, you will need to apply a tar base. This is then covered with a base wax. From this point on the waxing drill is basically the same for all sorts of ski surfaces.

1. Check the snow. The type of wax and the method of application depends on the snow state. Is it new or old, hard crust or powder, above or below freezing? The glove test (Page 35) is a good simple guide.

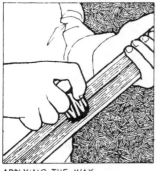

APPLYING THE WAX.

Fig. 9

SMOOTHING WAX WITH A CORK.

93

2. Select a wax, and READ THE INSTRUCTIONS on tube or can.
3. Wax indoors if possible, and be sure the skis are clean, dry and free from grit and old wax.
4. Apply the wax, covering the entire surface of the ski. The higher the temperature, the rougher the surface of the wax finish should be, so apply the wax roughly.
5. If you need good glide, cork the wax out smoothly.
6. Put the skis outside to adjust to the cold, and then *test your wax* by ski-ing around for a few minutes. If you have too much grip, cork the wax out some more. If not enough grip, put on some more wax, in a rough surface.

## KLISTERS

Klisters come in tubes, and to apply them successfully you need to warm up the tubes first, and then apply the klister indoors. Smooth out the klister with the heel of the hand. It's messy, but you can wipe your hands clean in the snow.

Put on a thin layer first, as removing klister is a difficult operation. You will also need some warmth to get the stuff off.

## BASE WAXES

Synthetic skis don't hold running waxes as well as wood, and you will need to apply a base wax to the synthetic to provide a binder for the running wax. You can get spray-on base wax preparations, or you can paint or melt base-wax on from a can.

## REMOVING THE WAX

The three common methods of removing waxes are:
1. By scraper.
2. By melting it off with a blowtorch.
3. By the use of solvents.

A scraper is a basic item, and which of the other two you use, depends on their availability. Don't spray solvents onto the ski. It is better to damp a soft rag and wipe it over the wax in order to remove it.

## WAXING AREAS

Because I believe it is better, I recommend that you wax the whole ski. Many authorities recommend that you need only wax the "kicking" area — that is the area under the foot, and indeed some synthetic skis have a marked scale in this waxing area to

SCRAPING OFF OLD WAX.    REMOVING WAX WITH BLOWTORCH

Fig. 10

help you remember how much of it you have covered. Others recommend a 'kicking' wax in this area, and 'glide' waxes on tip and tail. Many experienced ski tourers recommend using a paraffin glide wax in the ski groove, which collects ice, rather than a running wax. The permutations are endless, and the aim is the same — to ski cross-country with ease. Experience will teach you which method works best for you — so don't worry.

However, the beginner can avoid much of this waxing toil and expense if, initially anyway, he sticks to using Universal, or 'Wide-Range' waxes.

## WIDE RANGE WAXES

The basic idea of a wide range wax is that it cuts the waxing decisions down to one. Is it above or below freezing? Put another way, is the snow wet — (above 0°C) or dry — (below 0°C).

Wide range waxes reduce the calculations still further by naming the waxes in a simple fashion. Most major manufacturers have a wide range wax, for example:

| SNOW | TEMP | MANUFACTURER | | |
|------|------|------|------|------|
| | | REX | SWIX | TOKO |
| Wet | Above 0°C | Plus | Plus | Plus |
| Dry | Below 0°C | Minus | Minus | Minus |

It could hardly be easier!

## CHECKING THE SNOW

Most cross country ski-ers prefer to check the temperature by the state of the snow, rather than by using a thermometer, which just records the air temperature. Cross-country ski-ers use the glove test .

You pick up a handful of snow in your gloved hand and squeeze it. Open your hand and see what's happened.

1. A snowball has formed, or moisture on the glove = WET SNOW.
2. If the snow blows away = DRY SNOW.

It may sound crude, but for the touring ski-er it's quite adequate. Now all you have to do is select a wax, and put it on the ski. (See charts below).

If it has snowed overnight, or it is still falling, use this chart:—

### FALLING OR NEW SNOW

| SNOW STATE | MANUFACTURER | | | |
|---|---|---|---|---|
| | TOKO | SWIX | REX | RODE |
| Fine flakes | Olive or green | Green | Green | Green |
| Dry flakes | Blue | Blue | Blue | Blue |
| Forms a snowball (moist) | Red | Violet or Yellow | Violet or Yellow | Violet or Yellow |
| Leaves hand wet (wet) | Yellow or Red Klister | Yellow Klister | Red Klister | Red Klister |

If the snow is a day or two old it has settled, so use this chart:

### SETTLED SNOW

| SNOW STATE | MANUFACTURER | | | |
|---|---|---|---|---|
| | TOKO | SWIX | REX | RODE |
| Small grains | Green | Green | Green | Green |
| Large grains, lumps | Blue or Violet | Blue | Blue or Violet Klister | Blue |
| Forms wet snowball | Yellow | Blue or Violet | Red or Red Klister | Violet |
| Leaves hands very wet. | Red or Violet Klister | Red Klister | Red Klister | Red or Silver Klister |

After a few days, with warm days and freezing nights, the snows construction starts to break down; it has *metamorphised,* so you use this one:

## OLD (METAMORPHISED) SNOW

| SNOW STATE | MANUFACTURER | | | |
|---|---|---|---|---|
| | TOKO | SWIX | REX | RODE |
| Hard crust 'skare' | Blue Klister | Blue Klister | Blue | Red Klister |
| Crumbly granulated | Violet Klister | Violet Klister | Violet Klister | Blue or Violet Klister |
| Melting wet | Red Klister | Red Klister | Silver or Red Klister | Silver or black Klister |

Please note that these charts leave out the many variations: Light Greens — Special Blues etc., — also that where two colours appear in one box the second one is the one to use when the snow may be wetter, or melting.


## FIBREGLASS SKIS

For recreational or touring ski-ers, the whole ski should be waxed. Make a special job of the camber area under the foot for this is where the 'kick' takes effect. It does not matter in which direction you spread the wax, but remember that the wider you spread the wax, whatever its colour, the more grip you get. This may not be a snag, for you may *want* more grip with that wax. On the other hand the more you polish it on or cork it out, the more glide you get.


## NON-WAX SKIS

I find it necessary to put a paraffin "glide"-wax on my non-wax skis. Applied thinly, it helps on the flat and downhill, while otherwise the skis seem a little slow. I put this on the tail of the ski, behind the 'cut', and well forward on the "shovel" leaving a good gap so that it cannot work back into the 'cut'-section.

## WOODEN SKIS

Unless covered with a plastic or fibreglass coat, the base of the wood ski will have to be treated with tar to exclude the wet and damp. You can buy tars which you put on with a spray or brush, or tars which have to be melted (not burned) on to the wood ski base. Depending upon the amount of use you give them, wooden sole skis may need tarring once or twice a season.

The tar must be covered with a full length covering of base wax, and this is, in turn, followed by the running waxes.

## RUNNING IN

No wax will perform efficiently until it has been used for a little while. Don't expect much until you have covered say a quarter of a mile on skis, (.3 km.).

## ADVICE

The best piece of advice I have had on waxing was to use my eyes and if in doubt, ask. If you see someone motoring along, better than the rest, with great ease, ask him how he is waxed. Store up such advice for future use and don't be too embarrassed to ask for it.

Chapter 6

# TECHNIQUE
## MOVING, TURNING, STOPPING

The basic movement of cross country is the diagonal stride, or pas alternatif', as the French call it. Essentially it is a loping striding slide, the arms swinging forward, shoulders high and back, giving impetus to the stride.

Many experts define the diagonal stride as an extension of the normal walking movement, but it isn't as simple as that. To learn the knack I suggest you try out the following.

## DIAGONAL STRIDE

Find a flat piece of snow, up to 50 metres long, and position yourself at one end, skis parallel and about 6" (15 cm.) apart. Now start to walk across the snow, left leg first, swinging the right arm shoulder high, lifting and placing the right pole just forward of the right boot, the pole slanting back from the wrist.

Continue, swing the arms alternately, left leg,-right arm, right arm-left leg. Make a positive movement, and avoid weak swings which will end up with you swinging the right arm with the right leg!

After about six or seven paces when the arms are going well, lean forward, bend the knees and *kick* with the rear foot, sliding the first foot forward. This is a powerful skating movement, and you must take advantage of it, to prolong the glide as far as possible.

As you slide, bring the rear foot up with alternate arm, plant pole, kick, slide, alternate arm swing, plant pole, kick!—and you're off. **Two points:** Keep the arms swinging and the *knees bent*. You can't kick with a straight leg. And keep going, don't stop kicking.' **Two more points:** Don't plod. You can kick and slide quite slowly, but keep the movement going.

Fig. 11

You may find it easier to begin with if you practise without poles. They help balance and provide push, but they are something extra to think about. Try a few circuits without poles first, to get the arms swinging properly.

The diagonal stride is not dissimilar to a skating movement, but fore and aft. Once you get the idea — which should be the first time, if you follow these instructions, you will start to cover the ground quickly and easily, with firm kicks and long glides. But don't just kick and slide forward in the same position. Having kicked, the rear foot should be unweighted and coming through to glide, while the *other* leg kicks. Don't let the first kicking leg trail.

## POLE TECHNIQUE

Examine the diagram (Fig. 12) carefully. Note that the pole *slants to the rear.* Don't stab forward, as if to gain ground. The pole provides about twenty-five percent of your impetus if it is applied to the REAR, so don't waste the movement. Remember also to keep the arms at shoulder height apart, swinging them close to the sides. Don't spread them wide as this again wastes effort.

If you grip the poles tightly and heave yourself forward by the arms you will tire yourself out very quickly. Grasp the poles lightly, bearing down on the strap, and letting the grip slacken until, as you near the end of the movement, the pole is grasped between thumb and first finger, ready to swing forward.

Fig. 12

Fig. 13

## DOUBLE POLING

You can use this to gain speed while sliding or for extra impetus when doing the diagonal stride.

Swing both arms forward together, placing the poles firmly and swinging through to the rear. It's pretty tiring, but it can be useful when striding. Save effort by taking two kick and glide strides between each pole thrust. Use the weight of the body not the strength of your arms to power the poles back. (Fig. 13)

## TURNING

Stopped on the flat, you can just shuffle round, taking care not to let the tails or tips cross. It's not very graceful but it gets you there. On a slope you use the kick turn, which is also useful, as illustrated here (Fig. 14) for crossing obstacles.

## KICK TURNS

The secret of a successful kick turn is to plant the poles clear of the skis. The most simple rule is *'Plant the pole to the rear of the first ski you move.'* This will cover you for all eventualities, for you swing your ski round the planted pole, transfer the weight, and bring the other ski over.

Fig. 14

## SKATING TURNS

Next to the diagonal stride the skate turn is the most useful technique, and one you will need all the time. A neat skate turn gets you out of rutted tramlines, past a fallen friend, or round a tree. Time spent learning and practising it will not be wasted.

Let us assume a turn to the right. Start double poling and bend the knees. For a skate turn, be sure you are running on parallel skis. Transfer all your weight on the left ski, while you lift the right one which is then pointed off 45° into the new direction. Now kick off the left weighted ski, transferring the weight on to the right gliding one. Bring the left ski parallel and off you go in the new direction. Now try it to the left. (Fig. 15)

## STEM TURNS

It's important to remember that most cross-country skis have no metal edges. Therefore turns, especially the stem turn, must be executed by transferring the weight, and not by carving the turns, as you can do with heavy, edged downhill skis.

The stem is used for turning at the end of a traverse.

1. Run the traverse, skis apart, knees bent, weight evenly on the skis; turn point approaches.

2. Keeping the knees bent, transfer *all* the weight to the downhill ski.

3. Stem, by pushing out the rear of the upper ski, to make a wide 'V' of the tips.

4. Keeping the upper ski flat in the snow, transfer the weight on to it. Lean *out* as your body swings round.

5. Once round, the weight is still on the outside (downhill) ski. Bring in the unweighted upper ski, spread the weight evenly and continue the traverse. Repeat the process for the next turn (Fig. 16).

## STOPPING: SNOWPLOUGH STOP

You *can,* when you get very good, do jump turns in order to stop. Until then you will rely on the snowplough position to slow down, and stop you.

For this, the knees are bent, and the heels, well down on the heel plate are forced out, the ski tips making a 'V'. Keep the ski tips together and you will soon stop. Cross-country ski-ers are cautious about descending slopes without a good clear run out at the bottom. So now let's talk about climbing up and coming down.

Fig. 15

SKATE TURN

Fig. 16

STEM TURN

105

## Chapter 7

# GOING UP AND COMING DOWN

The uninitiated are amazed that the cross-country ski-er can, on the same wax, ski fast down hill, zip along the flat, and climb steep slopes. The secret lies in the waxing, good techniques, and in the effects of friction. When the ski is in motion, friction melts the snow under it, and gives glide. When the ski stops, this melting stops too, and you get adhesion, and adequate grip for kicking or climbing.

## CLIMBING

**Diagonal Stride:** The diagonal stride will get you up most reasonable slopes if you remember to keep the weight forward, and the knees bent.

Don't try for a long glide. Short, even strides will get you there, together with short thrusts from the poles. The crucial thing is to keep the weight forward and move on your toes.

**Running Stride:** A shorter, but steeper slope can be overcome by taking it at a run. Bound forward, throwing the weight from the rear to front ski, and your impetus will probably get you there. If not, you will have three remaining choices.

**(1) Side Stepping:** Start at the bottom, skis at right angles to the fall line, weight on lower ski and lift the upper ski to the side. Transfer the weight on to it. Bring up the lower leg. Repeat until you get to the top. (Fig. 17)

It is very important to keep the skis parallel to the fall line, or you can slide away forward or back.

**(2) Herringbone:** The Herringbone takes its name from the pattern the skis leave behind in fresh snow.

Facing the slope, point the skis out sideways, heels together in the reverse of the snowplough (Fig. 17). Keep the knees bent in together and climb the slope. The herringbone is much faster, but more tiring than the side step, but is useful for short steep slopes.

**(3) Traverse Turns:** Big wide slopes lend themselves to the traverse turns. Take the slope at an angle, and zig-zagging your way up, use alternative strides, single poled, for the traverse, and an uphill skating, or kick turn for the corners. You will need to edge the skis for the turns, or, if the slope is very steep or icy, use the kick turn across your own uphill tracks. (Fig. 18)

Fig. 17

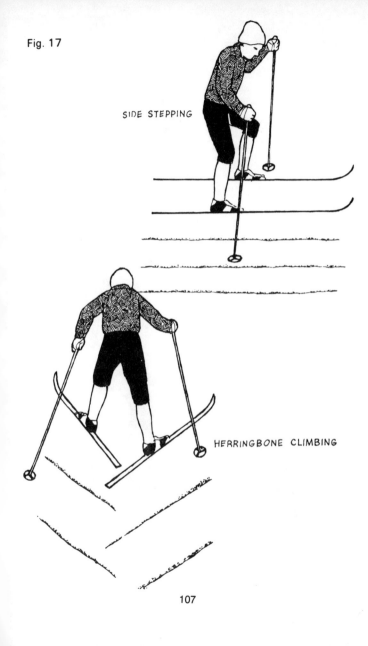

SIDE STEPPING

HERRINGBONE CLIMBING

Fig. 18

## COMING DOWN

**Schuss:** The easiest is the straight, skis parallel, downhill run. Stay upright, weight even on both feet, and let yourself go. Keeping the knees bent and holding the poles out at right angles to the body can help you to maintain balance while crossing bumps.

If your path takes you through trees or bush, remove the hands from the pole loops. If the basket catches on a branch you may drop the pole, but if your hand is in the loop you will get a badly wrenched arm as well.

**Traversing: Turning:** On a long steep slope, with a cluttered or obscured run out, run down the hill in a zig-zag traverse turning with the skate turn, or stem turn, on even slopes, or using the kick turn if the slope looks too steep.

**Telemark Turn:** The Telemark turn is a beautiful movement. You have all seen the Telemark position probably on television, for it is the position that ski jumpers adopt on landing. Knees are bent, rear leg trails, arms are held out wide. From this you can gather that the Telemark position looks and feels, very stable. The turn itself needs some two hours hard work on the slope to perfect. (Fig. 19)

Find an even slope, preferably with light snow cover, and go to the top.

1. Start down, with the knees bent, and with the skis slightly ploughed.
2. Slide one ski well ahead of the other, until the **binding** of the forward ski is level with the **tip** of the rear ski. All your weight is forward, the rear ski is trailing.
3. Keep the poles out at right angles to aid stability.
4. Now stem the forward ski slightly and you will go round in a wide graceful turn. If your right leg is in front you stem it out, to turn to the right.
5. Let the rear ski trail and remember that the rear leg is bent, and below the knee is parallel to the trailing ski.
6. Expect a few falls before you get the knack. Learning a Telemark turn is rather like learning to ride a bicycle. Once you get the hang of it you don't fall off so much!

Linked Telemark turns are an excellent way of descending a wide long open slope that is not too steep. You can build up a considerable speed on cross-country skis, **so be careful.**

Fig. 19

TELE MARK TURN

110

Fig. 20

WALL CROSSING

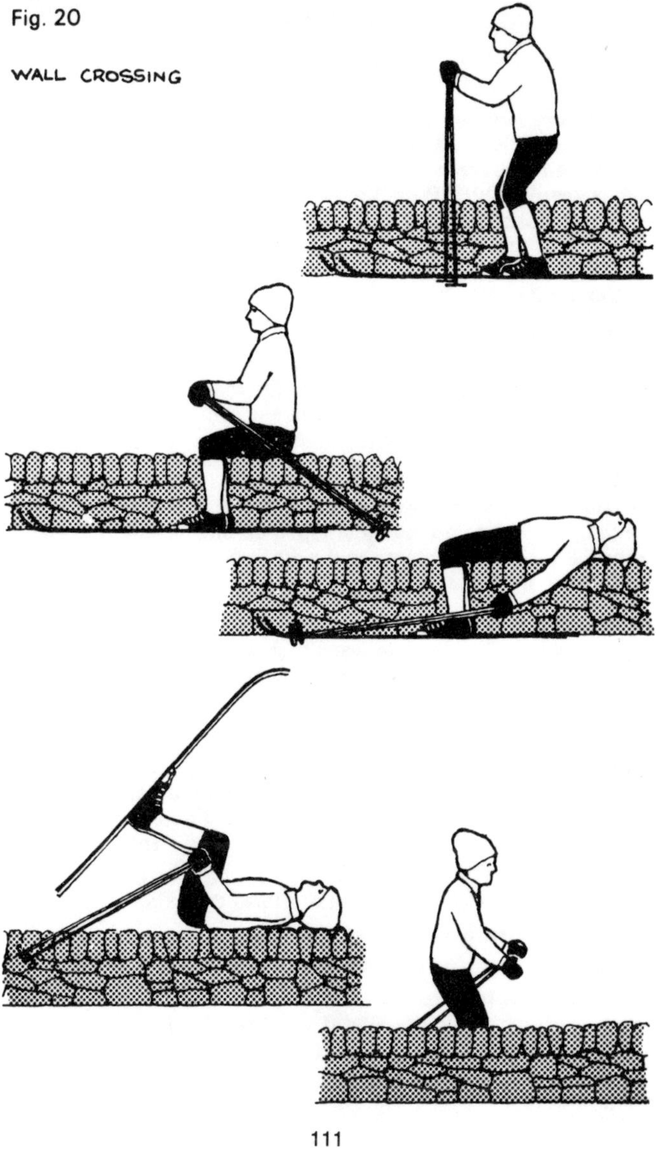

## Chapter 8

# OBSTACLE CROSSING

By its very nature cross-country ski-ing takes the ski-er up to obstacles. Since it is not always possible to remove the skis to cross them, the cross-country ski-er has evolved ways of doing so while keeping the skis on. Snow has often drifted deeply against walls and fences, so you must keep your skis on to avoid sinking. Remember that cross country equipment is light, so that given a little agility you will soon be able to perform these manoeuvres without difficulty.

## LOW FENCES
Use the kick turn. Stop parallel with the fence, and place one pole over on to the other side, level with the rear of the skis. Now lift the inner ski up, over, round and down. You are now straddling the fence. Bring the other leg over, and away you go. (Fig. 14)

## LOW WALLS
Stand parallel with the wall, and if it is snow covered, step up onto it. Now bring up the other leg, then one ski down, then the other. If the drop is greater on the other side, put the poles down and jump off, feet together.

## BACK ROLLS
If the wall is wide or up to waist high, try rolling over it on your back. Sit or lean back on the wall. Lie down on the top, lifting the skis, and roll over to put the feet flat on the far side. (Fig. 20)

## FENCE JUMP
For obstacles up to elbow height, try jumping. Find a fence post and stand parallel with the fence. Remove the hands from the pole straps and place the poles close to the outer ski. Place the other hand on the fence post, and swing between post and poles. Take a breath and:—

1. Swing up, bending the knees to raise the skis.

2. Jump round, twisting over the fence.

3. Land on both skis on the far side facing the other way.

As with the Telemark, it's a knack, and needs a little practice. Start with waist-high fences if you like. An obstacle crossing 'follow-my-leader' game, played to and fro over a fence, is the best way to get everybody going on this very useful XC skill. (Fig. 21)

Fig. 21

HUP!

## STREAMS

Be wary of streams. Don't splash across with your skis on, or they will ice up when you reach the snow. Try and find a snow bridge, but only if it is not too wide or the stream not too deep. Use fallen trees, or go higher up until the stream narrows. Use bridges—that's what they are for.

## ROADS

Don't forget to check if anything is coming. Step on to the road, and lift the feet high when crossing. Do not slither or you will scrape the wax off, or damage the surface of your non-wax ski.

## Chapter 9

# DAY TOURING

Let us assume that you have started your cross-country ski-ing, with a week's holiday. After three days instruction you should be ready to undertake a little tour. You won't be very expert, but you can get along, and one way to improve skill and build up stamina is to go for a day tour.

## EQUIPMENT

There must be at least three in the party. You need to carry, apart from normal clothes, skis and poles, a rucksack with the following items:—

1. Spare warm clothing.
2. Compass and map; (can you use them?)
3. Extra ski tip.
4. First aid kit.
5. Warm food in vacuum flask and/or
6. Food plus stove.
7. Whistle.
8. 'Space' blanket.
9. Matches.
10. Candles.

Take this, even for a half-day's outing. If you are going all day then you should also take:

11. Sleeping bags.
12. Light tent.

You may get stuck out overnight. Someone may get a touch of exposure. These items add little to your load—and in return take a bigger load off your mind.

However, if you are going on a short tour, on well marked and frequented trails, you may well decide to carry less. It is, however, as well to be prepared, and get in the **habit** of safety. This equipment spread among three or more people will hardly be noticed.

## ROUTES

Work out your routes beforehand, and prepare a route card. This simply notes the compass bearings and map references for each part of the trip, and puts in the timings. On skis your speed over similar distances can vary immensely from a few hundred yards in an hour to a speed of 20 mph or more. It depends on the terrain. Study the contours on the map and make calculated time estimates, noting these down on the route card.

Next, have your calculations checked, so that any error is noticed.

## SAFETY

Leave a copy of the route card behind, or placed somewhere visible in your car. If your party fails to return, someone will at least have an idea of where you might be.

## DAYLIGHT TIME

Remember that in winter, daylight hours are short, and often made even shorter in mountain country by changing weather or low cloud.

## DISTANCES

Cross-country ski-ing can be tiring work, so don't attempt too much to begin with. Remember that 10 km. out means another 10 km back, and that's 20 kms. Always choose a terrain and distance that is well within the capacity of the weakest member of the party. I recommend that you go no more than 8 km. (5 miles) out and back, until you are fitter, and confident in the snow.

## WAXES

It is quite likely that during the day, and by covering a distance, you will meet changing or totally different snow conditions. Take some spare waxes and a scraper.

## Chapter 10

# SNOW AND WINTER HAZARDS

The cross-country ski-er has to be far more concerned with the state of the snow than does the downhill ski-er. The downhill ski-er usually skis on prepared 'piste, regularly serviced by snow-cats or amtracks, and his heavier steel edged skis ride over or through ruts and ice which could disconcert the cross-country ski-er with his lighter equipment, who usually travels off-piste anyway.

Many places do, in fact, have prepared touring trails for the cross-country ski-er, over the hills and through the woods. Some even get provided with 'tramlines' to take the skis, but even here, because of the variation in terrain, and the presence of trees, the snow surface can change and this of course, affects the waxing. Finally, an understanding of snow is a useful aid when it comes to waxing itself.

## FALLING SNOW

Snowflakes are composed of crystals. One estimate has it that there are some 6000 different kinds of snowflake. Temperature decides the form they take while falling, and if it is warm, the crystals can jam up into large wet flakes, or if it is very cold, you can get the little soft pellets, or 'granules,' which are caused by the flakes falling through fog or cloud.

The state of falling snow can change even as it falls and wet (over 0°C) and dry (under 0°C) snow, can be contained in the same snowfall.

## NEW SNOW

Broadly speaking, snow is defined as 'wet' or 'dry' and can vary from 'very dry' which is very light and can be kicked up or swirled about like dust, to a heavy, clinging type, that soaks through your clothes, and will form a snowball if squeezed in the hand.

## METAMORPHISM

As soon as a snowflake hits the earth, it starts to change, and this change is one of a series, collectively referred to as *Metamorphism*. The first noticeable effect of this is that a fall of fresh snow, high and fluffy, will settle into a more even and cohesive mass within a few days. This is caused by the melting and fusing together of the original snow crystals. Powder snow develops up to three days *after a fall.*

As snow fall follows snow fall, each fall has different characteristics, and the temperature within each layer can vary. The lower layers, under pressure from above, are continually melting, and water vapour from below is extracted into the upper layer. The lower crystals are continually growing together, and changing shape, and this process is referred to scientifically as *constructive metamorphism*. They eventually form what are known as cup-crystals, which are quite large, up to half an inch long, and, naturally, cup-shaped.

This is a sketchy outline, but you can see a pattern of light, insignificant snow on the top, increasing as you go down to larger ice crystals at the bottom. These varying shapes are continually changing, but do not mix. It is as if fine sand was layered on top of gravel, which in turn rested on large pebbles.

The next stage, often found in early spring, is produced by the continual melting and refreezing of surface snow, which produces a coarse snow, often encountered on the sunny side of mountains.

## WIND AND SNOW

The wind blows the snow about, forming drifts, and also shapes the heavier snow, forming ridges and cornices on the edges of escarpments. The wind pressure and the movement thus created can melt the crystals, and they then refreeze into hard wind-slabs, and stepped snow faces. Drift snow in the lee of trees or rocks can be of quite different composition from the snow all about it, and is often deep and soft.

## SKARE

Hard, icy snow, rutted and wind driven, is often referred to as 'skare'. It is hard stuff to ski on, and calls for careful waxing.

A knowledge of snow, is the basis of snow craft, one of the fundamental skis needed by cross country ski-ers, and ski-mountaineers. Snow, apart from being our highway, and travel surface, is also our greatest hazard. The mountains, in winter, need to be treated with respect, and a knowledge of possible hazards will go a long way towards avoiding them.

"It's perfectly safe, as long as you remember it's dangerous."

A demolition instructor coined that useful phrase, when referring to plastic explosive, but it's a remark well worth remembering in connection with outdoor activities in winter.

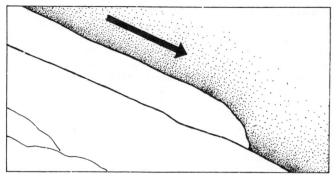

FLOWING AVALANCHE

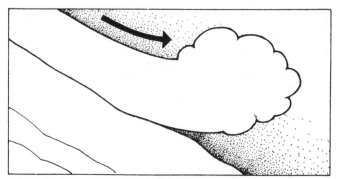

AIRBORNE POWDER AVALANCHE

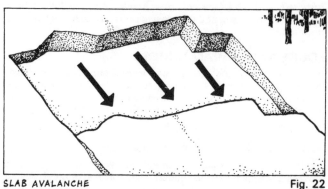

SLAB AVALANCHE

Fig. 22

119

## AVALANCHES (FIG. 22)

Most of the people killed or maimed by avalanches are ski-ers. Downhill ski-ers have some protection as they operate on prepared runs, under the watchful eye of local people and safety teams, who not only mark out safe runs, but remove impending dangers, often dislodging possible avalanches with dynamite. The best way to remove an avalanche is to create one, and the 'boom' of explosions doing just that, is a common sound in the mountains in winter.

## CARELESSNESS AND STUPIDITY

Most of the people killed every year are killed by carelessness. They ignore warning signs, ski round barriers, and run across avalanche slopes, often refusing to halt when ordered to. Even worse, sometimes the first ski-ers get away with it and their tracks, curving across that inviting slope, lure others out to their deaths.

NEVER:
1. Ignore avalanche warnings.
2. Ski past barriers, or on closed routes.
3. Ignore the advice of instructors, guides or avalanche teams.

Stress the danger to less experienced friends. Avalanches — make no mistake about it — are killers.

## TYPES OF AVALANCHE

Avalanches can occur almost anywhere. Tree-covered slopes, with a gradient of less than 15° can avalanche. People have been killed by avalanches less than 20 metres wide, flowing only a hundred yards. The snow collapsed under them, swallowed them up, settled over them and the pressure forced it to freeze, burying them alive.

## LOOSE SNOW AVALANCHES

After a fall of new snow, it can, as it settles, slip from the old base snow, and avalanche. Provided the rate of slide is slow, loose snow avalanches are not too dangerous, but if the slope is long and the speed builds up it can develop into the next, and very lethal, variety.

## AIRBORNE-POWDER AVALANCHE

In these, the snow gains momentum, flies into the air, and creates a terrific blast and suction. They travel at great speed, up to 200 mph and are amazingly destructive, shattering buildings, stripping trees from a slope, hurling buses and cars from roads. They are not unlike localized hurricanes. One such avalanche struck a busload of ski-ers in Switzerland and killed 24 out of the 35 on board.

## WET SNOW AVALANCHES

These are most common in the spring, when the snow melts. They tend to be slow, but heavy, and ski-ers caught in them will be crushed to death, but luckily they are slow, often follow regular routes, and occur at a predictable time of the year.

## SLAB AVALANCHES

These happen when a complete slab of snow breaks away in a unit, and plunges into the valley. They often occur on open grass slopes, and can come from snow packed into slabs by wind action.

Slab snow is always dangerous because the wind action has formed it into a mass, without having blended it to the surface beneath. It is therefore hanging up there by its own weight, and even the slightest pressure or movement can loosen it. Ski-ers are at particular risk from this sort of avalanche, for the snow looks so even and attractive that they are tempted on to it.

Stay off slab snow on open slopes.

## AVALANCHE PRECAUTIONS

The best precaution is to use common sense, listen to advice, and obey any signs or warnings.

Cross-country ski-ers, whose favoured terrain is country where avalanches occur, should travel in parties, and only cross slopes singly, having deployed an *oertal* cord behind them. An *oertal* cord is a length or red line, which you trail behind you. If you go under there is a good chance that this line will still be visible on the surface, and you can be located before you suffocate.

Before you cross a dodgy slope, try and test it first, by shouting, or throwing stones or snowballs out onto the snow. If nothing happens, loosen the ski bindings, remove the hands from the pole loops, and cross singly. Rope up the leader if possible.

If the slope carries someone away, watch where he disappears. If you feel the slope going get rid of skis and poles, for the snow wrenching them can fracture your arms and legs. Try 'swimming' to stay near the surface. Keep the mouth shut and as the slide slows, try and clear a space around the mouth and chest to give you breathing room.

Those on the surface should search the slope, and try and locate the victim first, before sending for an avalanche team. Speed is essential in avalanche rescue.

There is a lot more to avalanches and this outline is only designed to acquaint you with the danger, and probability. Perhaps this knowledge will come in useful one day. To learn more, I would recommend that you read Colin Fraser's excellent and readable 'Avalanche Enigma' (John Murray 1966), or if you prefer a fictional, but factually correct thriller, read Desmond Bagley's, 'The Snow Tiger' (Fontana 1976).

## WIND CHILL

The hills are windy, and cross-country ski-ing is warm work. This can lead to the ski-er taking inadequate precautions against the elements, which may be fine when you are moving, but is not to be recommended when you stop. In particular, beware of the wind-chill factor. The theory of wind-chill is founded on the fact that once the temperature gets below 0°C, any wind will intensify the effect of the cold, in direct ratio to its strengh. Observe the following chart.

**WIND CHILL CHART**

| Wind Speed | Local Temperature (F) | | | |
|---|---|---|---|---|
| 0 | 32 | 23 | 14 | 5 |
| 5 | 29 | 20 | 10 | 1 |
| 10 | 18 | 7 | −4 | −15 |
| 15 | 13 | −1 | −13 | 25 |
| 20 | 7 | −6 | −19 | 32 |
| 30 | 1 | −13 | −27 | 41 |

Note then, and don't forget, that the *effective* temperature can, thanks to the wind, be much lower than the true air temperature, and this can lead to such irritations as chapped skin, cracked lips, frost nip, and even more serious, frost-bite.

## FROST BITE

If you perspire, your undergarments and sweaters can get wet. Wet clothing, however it gets wet, loses its insulation.

Wet socks or sweat-soaked shirts are no protection, so change the first and cover up the second.

True frost-bite is not very common, but frost nip or the cracking of skin exposed to severe cold is quite prevelent. A good lip-salve or a barrier cream can help a lot.

To prevent frost-bite, maintain body warmth and avoid tight laces and constricting clothing. Stay dry. Wear wool, avoid synthetics, and keep the extremities, feet, toes, fingers, nose and ears, protected and warm.

## TREATMENT

The frosted part will go white and feel dead. Warm the affected part slowly, with body warmth. Fingers can be held in the mouth or under the armpit, toes can be held under a friend's sweater. Never rub the affected part directly, least of all with snow.

Restore warmth slowly. If a warm bath is available start with tepid water and warm it gradually. Never rush the re-warming process.

As with avalanches, be aware of the danger. Frost-bite may be rare, but the effects are unpleasant.

## EXPOSURE (Hypothermia)

The condition referred to as 'exposure' is caused by inadequate protection against cold, wet and wind. On their own, neither of these three need bother the ski-er. In combination they can be lethal. Hypothermia, which can be the end result of exposure, is severe loss of body heat, and can cause death.

Prevention is the best answer. Correct clothing, regular food, and adequate rest, will avoid exposure. The symptoms of exposure come on slowly at first, then with increasing severity and rapidity. Uncharacteristic stumbling, speaking in a slurred voice, becoming withdrawn, stupidity, or sometimes sudden bursts of chatter, listlessness, may be signs of exposure — don't shrug them off. Once the victim collapses you have a severe problem.

## TREATMENT

STOP and get out of the wind. If the victim is in the early stages and conscious, get him or her warm. Make a shelter or form a windbreak. Dry the casualty and get him into dry clothes. Cover up the head and hands — thirty per cent of the body's heat loss is from the head — give him a hot drink from the vacuum flask. If possible get him into a space blanket or sleeping bag. However, if you are on a day tour you probably won't have one, but a large plastic bag is an excellent substitute, particularly if it's large enough for someone else to get in beside the victim, to create extra warmth.

If the victim is unconscious, then the situation is very serious and medical aid should be obtained as quickly as possible. Do not force any drinks into an unconscious person. Place the victim in the Recovery Position (Fig. 23). The basic rule in cases of exposure is to re-warm the victim as fast as is reasonably possible, while cutting out the elements which caused the condition to arise. So, shelter, rest and warmth are the answers.

## GETTING LOST

Never go into the hills or mountains in winter on your own. There should be at least three people in the party, you should carry overnight gear — just in case, and leave a note of your intended route behind.

Every member should have a local map and compass and know how to use it.

If you are sensible, and have a sound grasp of outdoor skills, you will find in cross-country ski-ing the activity for a lifetime.

Fig. 23

THE RECOVERY POSITION

# Part 3

# Parallel Skiing

## Chapter 1

# GETTING THE BASICS RIGHT

**Why** can't you parallel ski? What **exactly** is the problem? Others can do it, drat them, so why not you? That's the first question you must ask yourself, and your instructor, and be sure you get an answer from each. Let me give you a personal illustration.

After a day falling headlong down the slopes of Austria, very tired, and with all confidence gone, I asked my instructor which was the **biggest** mistake I'd made all day. He thought for a minute and said, **"Well Rob, I don't think getting up this morning was a very good idea!"**

Very funny! However, when pressed, we discussed my lack of fitness and fear of the fall-line, and the tendency to over-edge in the turn. My skis—at 210 cm, were too long, and so were my poles. I changed to 185 cm skis and had 10 cms cut off each pole.

By now incensed, I marched into the ski-shop and cornered the boot-expert. He tore off my boots and two pairs of thick socks, and my boot size fell from 11 to 9! I went to bed early, and decided that the stem-turn days were over. The next day I invested in some private lessons, and happily, I can now parallel ski.

Let's just think this story over, for there are lessons here.

Firstly, without good fitting boots, you won't be able to learn parallel ski-ing. You won't have the control. With the incorrect length of ski or over-long poles, you are just making difficulties for yourself. If you stay up all night or go ski-ing completely unfit, with weak legs, then steep mogul slopes will tire you before your technique develops sufficiently.

Finally, determination. You may, gentle reader, be a natural downhill, gung-ho, hot-rodder. In which case you have wasted the price of this book. However, if you are the normal timorous mortal who views awful drops with natural reservation, then you may prefer to stay on easy slopes and stick to gentle stems.

The problem is that with this you can't go very far. You must parallel to go high where the great ski trails are. Sooner or later, however much you dislike the prospect, you must point those skis down the slope and learn to parallel. So **determination** is an important factor whether you summon it early or late.

Finally, a word of comfort. Once you tackle steep slopes, they seem to flatten out. Fear, once tackled, ebbs away. It really is quite easy. All you have to do is try.

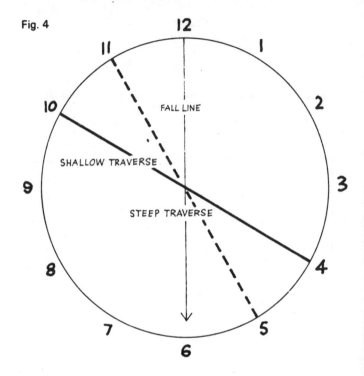

Fig. 4

12 · 1 · 2 · 3 · 4 · 5 · 6 · 7 · 8 · 9 · 10 · 11

FALL LINE

SHALLOW TRAVERSE

STEEP TRAVERSE

## STARTING POINT

We are going to assume that you have some ski-ing experience, and can perform the following basic manoeuvres, which have been outlined in Basic Ski-ing: traversing, the snow plough turn, side-slipping etc. These elements, with others we are about to learn, will form part of your parallel turns.

Now you need a slope. Choose one with an angle of about 45°, as wide as possible, and with a good run out at the bottom. To give direction and traverse angle, we will use the "clock" system i.e. a shallow traverse, left to right, will be from 10 o'clock to 4 o'clock. A steep one would be from 11 o'clock to 5 o'clock.

128

Chapter 2

# THE STEM TURN

We are going to get the basics right, and the basic turn on a steep slope is the stem turn.

## STARTING POSITION
Get into the traversing position, skis together, upper ski in front, weight on downhill ski, skis edged into the slope. Now:-

Point the skis MORE down the slope. However much you **want** to point them, however much you usually point them down, point them MORE. The turn will then be easier.

Hold the poles lightly, at shoulder width, and push off, looking straight ahead, and well across the slope, not just a few metres ahead. Look and think DOWNHILL. Face the fact of the slope and get used to it.


## THE TURN (Fig. 2)
For the basic stem, you move from the traverse position as follows:

DO

1. Bend the knees.

2. Open out the uphill ski, to make a 'V' with the lower one.

3. Transfer your weight gradually on to the 'V'd uphill ski. You will start to turn downhill.

Now, this is the point where you formerly gave up, and sat down backwards, or fell over, out of the turn—DON'T: Instead:

DO

4. Lean forward, and look out of the turn.

By so doing, the turn will continue round and you will again be traversing the slope, weight on the now outer downhill ski.

DO

5. Slide the upper ski in to the traverse position.

6. Correct your traverse position and go STRAIGHT INTO ANOTHER TURN.

Now if you descend the slope, practising the stem, in a series of linked turns, for say one hour, you will, firstly, improve your stemming and secondly realise that it's still not quite right. The time has come for a few refinements.

TRANSFER THE
WEIGHT GRADUALLY
ONTO THE OUTSIDE
SKI

BEND THE KNEES
STEM OUT THE
UPHILL SKI

**Fig. 2**

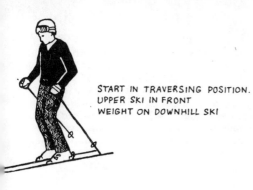

START IN TRAVERSING POSITION.
UPPER SKI IN FRONT
WEIGHT ON DOWNHILL SKI

NOW
SLIDE THE
UPPER
SKI IN

## COMMON ERRORS (Figs. 3-6)

Failing to **bend the knees** before the turn is a very common error, and one with woeful consequences. With bent knees, you can press out on the outer ski, and induce the turn, tightening it if necessary as you cross the fall-line. So, bend the knees.

But, and it's a big but, when pressing out for the turn, **never allow the outer leg to get straight,** with the knee locked. If you do, your weight will fall inward, and you will **either** over edge, with the inner edge of the outer ski hooking you round, or full back into the turn. Use your weight, not your muscle.

Turning with a stiff outside leg is a common and major fault. Keep the outer knee bent and the weight between the hips.

DO

Keep the body evenly between the skis, knees bent, pressing out the turn, and letting the weight drift across as you cross the fall-line.

Swinging the shoulders round when attempting to induce the turn is another common error, so,

DO

Keep the shoulders square, and keep the skis on the snow. This will give you a good gliding turn.

## SPEED

You may find, when traversing the slope that, because of your steeper line, you are going too fast for comfort. Side-slip to lose speed, before straightening up for the turn. **Don't** stem out, after a side slip, with the tips pointing **uphill,** or you won't get round.

Now re-read this section on Errors, and carry on practising. Once the Stem has been perfected, you will be less worried about the fall-line, and ready for another turn. Spend at least one hour refining your traverse position, side slipping and stem turns. Take it in turns, each correct the other's error. **Never** do just one turn always do at least **three.**

## GIVING ADVICE

Unless something is **very** wrong, don't shriek advice at your partner when he (she) is attempting a turn. They either won't hear you, or, distracted, in attempting to correct what they have just done they will get something else wrong. Discuss **major** errors after each attempt. If you get the major error corrected, many minor errors will cease to occur.

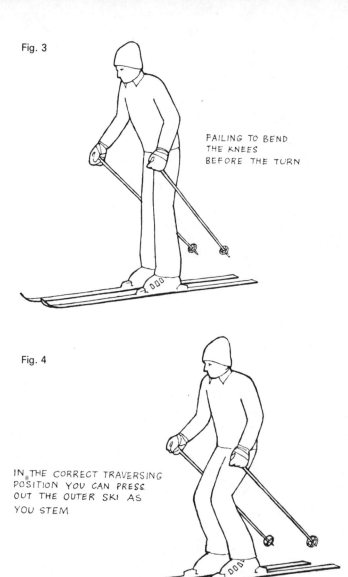

Fig. 3

FAILING TO BEND
THE KNEES
BEFORE THE TURN

Fig. 4

IN THE CORRECT TRAVERSING
POSITION YOU CAN PRESS
OUT THE OUTER SKI AS
YOU STEM

133

Fig. 5

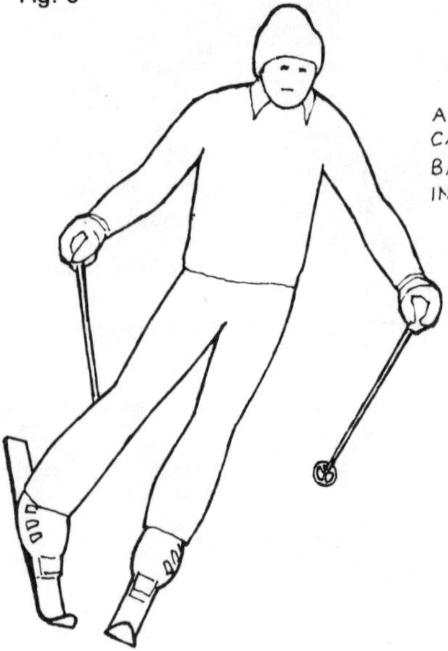

A STIFF OUTSIDE LEG
CAUSING YOU TO
BALANCE ON THE
INSIDE SKI

ANOTHER CONSEQUENCE OF
A STIFF OUTSIDE LEG —
AN EXCESSIVE STEM

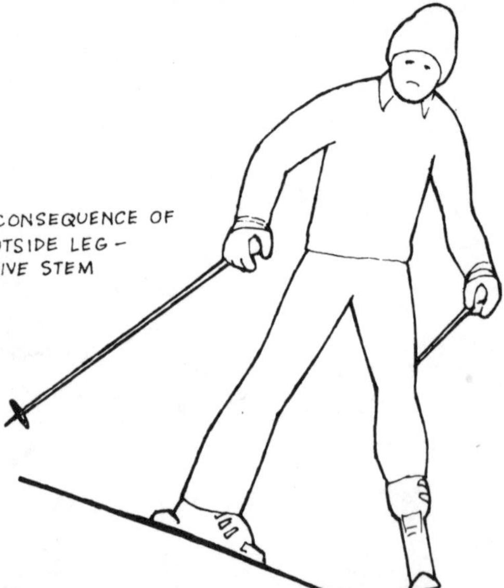

Fig. 6

## Chapter 3

# UPHILL STOP CHRISTIES

So far, we have worked on perfecting the traverse and stem turn. This involves moving the uphill ski out to form a V. We must now start learning to turn with the skis together and the best way to learn is to turn UPHILL.

This turn is a useful step in the progressive learning of parallel ski-ing, for it involves more elements, and is also useful for increasing confidence, as it is a stopping movement, useful on the steepest slopes, where you may be afraid that, once under way, you cannot stop.

## STARTING POSITION

This turn is easier on steeper slopes and with a steeper line. Get in the traverse position and head across the slope on a steep incline, 10 to 4, or better still 10 to 5 (see Fig. 1).

**The turn:**
1. Bend the knees.
2. Press the knees into the slope, thus edging the skis. Keep the skis together.
3. Keep facing down the slope.
4. Press out on the skis, **from the bend knees,** flattening them as you do so.
5. As the legs straighten you will turn up the slope, and stop.

Notice the importance of the bent knees at the start. If you do not bend the knees **before** the turn, you won't be able to press out on the skis, and round the turn out.

This turn should be practised **many times** at ever steeper angles.

## COMMON ERRORS

The most common error is swinging the shoulders up the hill, to induce the turn.

Study the points and the diagram (Figs. 7 & 8) and when turning, keep looking down the slope, pressing out the turn from the knees.

At this stage, don't induce the turn by planting the pole but concentrate on turning by flexing the legs and pressing out the turn, pushing the snow away from the underside of your skis.

PRESS KNEES
INTO THE SLOPE
EDGING THE SKIS

PRESS OUT
AND FLATTEN SKIS
UNWEIGHTING

Fig. 7

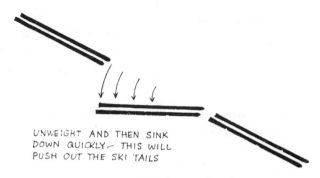

UNWEIGHT AND THEN SINK
DOWN QUICKLY — THIS WILL
PUSH OUT THE SKI TAILS

**Fig. 8**

## STOPPING AT SPEED

Your control and confidence will grow, if you intersperse the uphill stop-christies with skidded stop turns, commenced with a side slip.

Employ this turn when you feel the speed before the turn is excessive.

**Drill:**

1. From a steep traverse, flatten the skis into a side slip.

2. As the speed falls, bend the knees, lean forward and press the knees into the slope, and as the skis come round,

3. Keep the body facing downhill and come to a stop.

Please re-read this carefully, study the drawings and practise this manoeuvre many times, to right and left.

The turn involves:

1. Keeping the skis parallel.

2. Bending and flexing the knees.

3. Keeping the body facing downhill throughout the turn.

4. Pressing out the skis.

Item 2 will form the basis of the next chapter, when we learn the basics of unweighting the tails of the skis, an essential requirement for the parallel turn.

It is extremely important to keep the body mobile. Don't stand on your skis, stiff and erect. **Flex** and **bend,** through the turn.

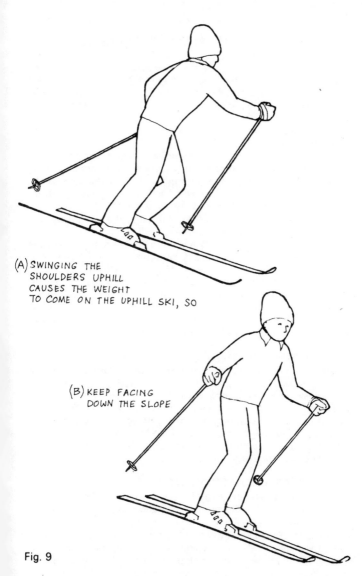

(A) SWINGING THE
SHOULDERS UPHILL
CAUSES THE WEIGHT
TO COME ON THE UPHILL SKI, SO

(B) KEEP FACING
DOWN THE SLOPE

Fig. 9

Chapter 4

## UNWEIGHTING: FLEXING: EXTENSION

Good ski-ers ski well because they use their weight, balance and technique, to master the slopes at speed. The beginner finds it very difficult to control his skis, not because they are heavy and awkward, but because the ski-er has not learned to control them.

### UNWEIGHTING (Fig. 10)

The boots hold the feet and the bindings link boot and ski. If you stand on the skis, and throw your weight from the bent knees up and forward, you will, momentarily, **unweight the tails of the** skis. Thus unweighted, they will easily turn, especially if unweighting linked to a pole and leg movement.

This method of "unweighting" throwing the weight **up** and **forward** is called "upwards unweighting".

It is possible, and some say easier, to unweight the skis by the reverse method, "downward unweighting", and some who normally ski with an upright stance will find this more natural.

For "down unweighting", from the upright stance on the skis, let the knees flex while throwing the weight down and forward which also has the effect of **unweighting the tails of the skis.**

So find a steep slope and run a steep traverse (11 to 5) into an uphill stop christie, and let us practise the unweighting.

### UPWARD UNWEIGHTING

**Position:** Keep the knees well bent, the weight forward, the hands forward at shoulder width. Don't be afraid to move fast, you know how to stop remember. THINK downhill.

**Turn:** Flexing the knees to give more spring, throw the weight forward and UP. Imagine your chest getting **over** the tips of your skis. Bend the knees into the slope, and you will skid round into the turn, the shoulders swinging out, to face down the slope. Press out the turn, and stop.

### DOWNWARD UNWEIGHTING

**Position:** Adopt an upright stance, body loose and knees slightly bent. Ride across the slope easing out the bumps until you reach the turning spot.

**The Turn:** Bend the knees and throw the shoulders forward over the boots, to shift the weight from the tails to the tips of the skis. Bend the knees into the slope and skid round into the turn,

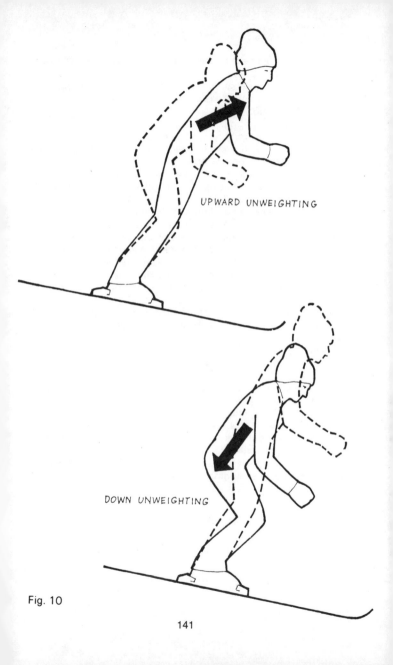

UPWARD UNWEIGHTING

DOWN UNWEIGHTING

Fig. 10

141

straightening the knees to press out the turn, and, stop as usual, facing down the slope.

Please note that these two methods have only one object: to unweight the skis and make it possible to turn them **together without stemming**.

Practice unweighting by both, or either method, for unweighting is essential to successful parallel ski-ing.

**Flexing:** The legs are the engines of the downhill ski-er, and they have to pump. Poor ski-ers don't use their legs. They simply stand on the skis and let the slope take control.

Let your legs drive you over the ground, flexing and extending, ironing out the shocks, driving the snow away from the base of the ski, and powering you into and through the turns.

**Extension:** The movement of the body, from the crouched traverse to the forward unweighted position, is called "extension". Extension, up and forward, will unweight your skis.

**A Point to Remember:** Many inexperienced ski-ers find flexing and extension difficult because either they don't understand why they are doing it, or are in the wrong position to begin with.

So remember: The object of flexing and extension is to unweight the skis, but you will be unable to flex or extend if you have already done so! Flexing and Extension are **movements,** not **positions.**

Unless you have a crouched traverse position **before** the turn, you will not be able to unweight during it, for unless you are **down,** you can't go **up.** If you are **up** you can't go **down**—got it?

If you are **up,** in an uphill stance, you can **only** use the downward unweighting.

Read this again—it is very important.

You must use your legs and body, in a continual flowing, flexing and extending movement.

Watch those experts and see how they flow down the slopes. It is the flexing and extending that gives that graceful line.

Chapter 5

# THE STEM CHRISTIE

The stem christie is, for the great majority of holiday skiers, THE turn. Most skiers never get beyond this turn, and if they are to progress, then a perfect stem-christie is a necessary step.

## STEM TURN AND STEM CHRISTIE (Fig. 11)

The stem-christie differs from the stem turn in many respects and, if you attempt a stem turn under certain conditions, it will speedily develop into a stem christie.

Compared with the stem turn, a stem christie is:

1. Faster.

2. Closer to the fall-line (10 or 11 to 5)

and

3. Has a smaller and shorter lasting stem.

Read this again. Then:

**Starting position:**

1. Traverse the slope, **at a steep angle to the fall-line**—running across towards **4** or **8,** then

DO

2. Flex the knees, lowering the body, upper ski in front, weight on downhill ski and . . .

DO

3. Stem out slightly and . . .

DO

4. Come up.

As you cross the fall-line, **bring the skis together.** By coming up at speed, you **will have unweighted the tails** and the movement will be easy. Once across the fall-line,

DO

5. Flex down and forward.

DO

6. Weight onto downhill ski, and press out to complete the turn.

DON'T

Make too wide a stem: You will either go into a plough, or fall out of the turn. (Fig. 9, Page 139).

CLOSE THE INNER SKI TO
THE OUTER SKI

Fig. 11

STEM OUT
SLIGHTLY

LOWER THE BODY AND
PLANT THE POLE

**DON'T Lean into the Slope:** This is caused by fear. If you are catching your inside edge, then you are leaning into the slope. Lean out. Keep the skis flat. Use your weight, don't carve away with those edges.

**Fall Backwards:** When you are on the fall-line, skis together, you speed up. This gives you a nasty moment, and you will either:

1. Fall over backwards, or

2. Stem out wildly, flinging your shoulders round and skid round to end up facing across or up the slope, skis ploughed. Are you doing this? (See Fig. 6. Page 134).

If so: your weight is wrong. You are leaning back (away from that slope) because you are afraid.

Your weight should, at this moment, be down and forward, evenly over the skis, the knees flexed, ready to press you out round in the turn. Finally, DON'T:

**Fall Out of the Turn:** As the turn steepens or just as you cross the fall-line, you catch the outside edge, and fall out across the outer ski.

This is usually caused by allowing the outer leg to get straight or by attempting to stem round the turn, rather than by using the weight and flexing.

DO

1. Keep the skis flat on the snow.

You can see the snag with perfecting the stem christie. There is a lot to do, and it all happens very quickly.

Notice, however, the basic points:

1. Steep angle to fall-line.

2. Down–up–down motion of the body into and through the turn.

3. **Slight** stem out, and weight transferred onto outer ski.

4. Look down the slope—always.

Now if you practise this, you will soon find that you are getting very fluid turns, and that the body movement gives you full freedom to turn the skis out.

## COMMON PROBLEMS

**Too much Speed:** Speed helps you in the turn, but you can have too much of it. Control your speed by little slide slips while traversing, but go steeply into the turn—slowly if you must, but **steeply.**

**Fear of the Fall-line:** Start on even slopes, and find steeper ones as your skill and confidence develop. Fear of the fall-line is

THE SHOULDERS SHOULD BE ACROSS THE FALL LINE AS YOU CROSS IT AND ANGLED TO FACE DOWNHILL THROUGHOUT THE TURN

TURNING THE DOWNHILL SHOULDER UP THE SLOPE IS A COMMON ERROR

**Fig. 12**

very natural and common, but it must be overcome. Be aware that fear is your problem and face it. It is very noticeable how a skier's skill and confidence improves **after** a fall. It doesn't hurt, and, that out of the way, you can concentrate on tackling the errors.

## COMMON ERRORS

1. Not bending the knees.

A very common error is to stem out, go round, into the fall-line with the skis apart, and then lift the inner ski over. Your outer leg is locked straight, and you are leaning in. It looks ungainly and it will result in a fall. Keep the skis close together, weight evenly between them, and slide the skis into line.

2. **Shoulders:** Keep your shoulders angled, across the skis, and across the slope. Your shoulders should be across the fall-line as you cross it, and angled to face downhill at all other times.

**Common Errors:** The common error is to try and turn the downhill shoulder UP the slope. In fact, you turn the uphill shoulder down the slope, and lead with it. Study the diagram (Fig. 12) and you will see how your shoulders should look.

**Practice:** The stem christie needs a lot of practice, and if you work on it for say half a day, descending slope after slope, time after time, getting each part right, one skier correcting the other after each series of linked turns, you will certainly improve.

Never do just one turn and stop. Do three. Then you will start on the opposite traverse. Read this chapter at least once before each full descent, and resolve to get another part refined, without forgetting the others, on each attempt.

This improved, if not perfected, you can proceed to the parallel turn itself.

## Chapter 6

# THE PARALLEL TURN

**Pole Planting:** At this level—beginning the parallel turn, the beginner is so anxious to go round with his skis together that he lets all else go hang. **DON'T.**

Also at this stage, the poles are used, and as their use is important to a successful parallel, we want you to understand that planting the poles correctly is an essential part of the parallel turn.

Read and observe the following points closely:

1. When heading into the turn, hold the arms slightly away from the body, elbows bent, and fists forward of the knees. The poles are slanted to the rear, baskets just behind the heels.

2. Approaching the turning point, swing the pole forward GENTLY from the WRIST.

3. **Plant the downhill pole vertically, by flexing the knees.**

Let us examine Point 3 more closely. Read it again. That is what you DO.

You DO NOT

1. Reach forward with the pole as if spearing a piece of paper. Or

2. Plant the pole by dropping the shoulder.

By flexing the knees as you plant the pole, you are putting yourself into the "ready to unweight" position—now do you see the idea?

If you find this difficult, a good tip, especially on steep slopes, is to ski with **very** short poles. This forces you to bend the knees just to get the pole in, and, even more important, reminds you that flexing is necessary.

3. Plant the pole vertically, about midway between the boot toe and the ski-tip. This spot will vary according to your height, but that is the general area.

So, once again:

1. Hold the poles gently to the rear while traversing.

2. Swing the downhill pole forward from the WRIST until vertical.

3. Plant the pole by flexing the knees, midway between boot and ski tip.

We now have you at the turning spot, angled steeply to the fall-line, flexed and with the pole planted.

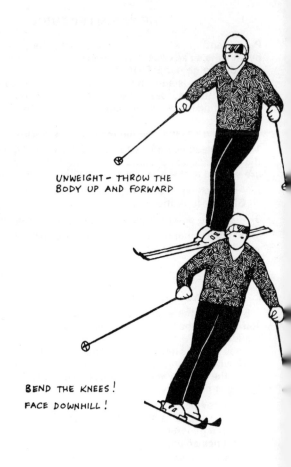

UNWEIGHT - THROW THE
BODY UP AND FORWARD

BEND THE KNEES!
FACE DOWNHILL!

**Fig. 13**

PLANT THE POLE BY
FLEXING THE KNEES

TAKE A STEEP LINE

DOWN AGAIN READY FOR
ANOTHER TURN

TRAVERSE

What do you do now?

UNWEIGHT—UNWEIGHT—UNWEIGHT!

1. Throw the body from the chest up and forward, flexing the downhill wrist.
2. Round you go. Keep the skis together and flat on the snow.
3. As you go round:
   1. Lean out and face downhill.
   2. Bend the knees flexing down, weight now on the downhill ski.
   3. Press down with the heels, hips into the hill, to side-slip if necessary. Traverse position again. Keep going, and straight into another turn.

DON'T (Fig. 14)

1. Stem the outer ski.
2. Lift the inner ski off the snow and step round.
3. Let the hips come forward.
4. Let the downhill shoulder lead.
5. Let the outer leg get stiff and locked.
6. Lean back.

DO

1. Think DOWNHILL—not a few metres ahead but for the bottom of the slope. Unweight positively—not feebly, and,
2. Keep the body loose and flexing.
3. Keep the skis on the snow.
4. Keep the weight between the skis.
5. Do more than one turn, do, or attempt to do at least **three** linked turns, never push out and stop.
6. Keep at it.

The parallel turn is like riding a bike. There is a knack to it, with lots of do's and dont's and it depends, like riding a bike, on weight, speed and confidence.

**How to practise:** Find a slope or part of the piste, that is at least 25% steeper than you like. Go to the top and note three turning points in the slope, at 5 o'clock, 8 o'clock and 5 o'clock repeating in a line, one to another down the slope.

Look DOWN the slope. You are going to go DOWN, not across or to and from, but DOWN.

152

Fig. 14

DO NOT REACH
FORWARD WITH
THE POLE OR
DROP THE SHOULDER

DO NOT STEM
THE OUTER SKI

DO NOT
LEAN BACK

DO NOT LEAD
WITH THE
DOWNHILL
SHOULDER

If you can, it is sometimes better to mark the turning points with twigs, or slalom poles, or even spare clothing. This gives you a definite point to turn round, and can be helpful.

Read the sections on the turn carefully, and make your run, through three turns at least, without stopping.

Concentrate on the Major points:

1. Planting the pole correctly, flexing.

2. **Unweighting.**

3. Skis together.

4. Looking downhill.

Get the major points right and many smaller ones will be overcome at the same time. Get your friends to comment on the points of your turns, good as well as bad.

Then let them descend, and by observing and commenting on their errors and noting their good points, the elements of the turn will start to break down, to you as well.

## SPEED

The parallel turn is a fast turn. You may find, initially, that even though you don't like the slope or the speed, you need speed to get round.

This is due to poor unweighting techniques. As you practise and as your fear is overcome, you will notice that you **seem** to be turning more slowly.

Actually, you are overcoming the fear of the slope and your brain is adapting to the manoeuvre. Once this starts, you will be able to refine the turn, correcting all the little details.

You will also be able to parallel on shallower traverses, since your improved technique will enable you to swing the skis through a wider arc.

# Chapter 7

## PARALLEL EXERCISES

As you will have realised, parallel ski-ing is not so easy and needs a certain dexterity. It requires, apart from specific technique, precise movements of the skis, the legs and the body.

Each little skill you acquire will help your control and increase your confidence. The following exercises can be tried if you cannot seem to master a complete turn, no matter how you try. They can be employed, just for practice or fun, by ski-ers of quite moderate ability. The exercises break down the basic elements of parallel turns.

**Tail Hopping:** Unweighting the tails of the skis is an essential part of parallel ski-ing.

To practise tail-hopping, run an even traverse, on the 4 or 8 o'clock line, and

1. Flex the knees, lean forward.

2. Throw the weight up and forward, and

3. Hop up, the heels of the skis clear of the ground.

4. After each hop, flex the knees and crouch.

5. Repeat.

Run several traverses, hopping as high and as often you can, flexing afterwards. If your heels are lifting and your skis are on the snow, tighten your clips or get smaller boots. Remember you must flex if you want to extend. So flex-up-flex-up-flex-up—and keep it going.

**Tail Hopping on the Fall-line:** This is the same exercise as the one above, but done directly down the fall-line. Look at the bottom of the slope, and try and throw the weight up and forward **from the chest.** Always sink into a forward flexed position after each hop. If you don't do this, you won't be able to hop—you can't go **up** if you already **are** up.

**Pole Planting with Flexing:** Run a traverse, or down the fall-line, under the eye of a critical friend, watching for correct pole planting technique.

1. Start in a fairly upright stance, poles slanted to the rear.

2. Swing the poles forward, and plant them vertically BY FLEXING the knees—NOT by dropping the shoulders. Do not let the pole go forward from the vertical line.

3. Repeat across or down the slope and keeping practising.

**Slalom:** Competition is a great spur. If you get the chance to enter the Friday races,. do so. If slalom poles are left on the slopes, by running a course through them, your turns will tighten up remarkably, and equally important, unless you get it right, you won't make the next gate. So try slaloming at any opportunity.

**Fear:** Knowledge dispels fear. That is the motto of the Parachute School. Think about what you are doing and dispel fear of the slopes or speed, by concentrating on what you are doing.

Just for the record, my instructor overcame my own, fairly well engrained fear of heights and steep slopes by a direct and somewhat brutal method.

After about half an hour, he stopped and said "You are afraid". "Fear is making you a bad ski-er". (It sounded better in French).

FLEX THE KNEES
LEAN FORWARD

THROW THE WEIGHT
UP AND FORWARD
HOP THE SKI TAILS
CLEAR OF THE SNOW

## *TAIL HOPPING*

Fig. 15

He then proceeded to send me down terrible slopes, straight schuss. It was quite nasty, and the descent was made at speeds where to fall would be even nastier, so somehow or other I stayed on my feet. After spending the rest of the morning going down one steep slope after another, I was exhausted, but no longer scared. I don't recommend this method, but if all else fails, you might care to try it.

### FIG. 16

**Pole Planting with Tail Hopping:** Link the above two exercises into one, first across the slope, then down the fall-line. If you slightly "over-cook" a hop on the fall-line, you will be into a 'wedel', so let it happen and keep it up as long as you can.

**Flexing and Unweighting:** This is a very beneficial exercise, on the schuss or traverse.

From an upright stance, unweight **up** and flex **down;** Up, down flex, up, down flex.

REPEAT

SWING THE POLE FORWARD
AND PLANT BY FLEXING
THE KNEES

# POLE PLANTING AND TAIL HOPPING

**FIG. 17**

**Side Hopping:** This is the last exercise you can reasonably do, without going into a full turn.

Running a traverse, you can hop up, trying to land the ski tail above or below your pre-hop breakpoint.

Since this is an awkward manoeuvre it has useful training advantages.

To stay upright, you will have to flex, or edge, or flatten the skis quickly on landing. This will make you nimble and responsive to the results of your actions.

PLANT THE POLE
VERTICALLY WITH THE
FOREARM PARALLEL
TO THE SNOW

REPEAT

**Fig. 16**

Fig. 17

SIDE HOPPING

## SHORT CUTS
Personally, I am not sure that there are any real short cuts. You need to know what you have to do, and go out and practice until you can do it. Private lessons will help, and can be recommended.

Chapter 8

# MOGULS

Moguls are bumps. Big, uneven craters, and mounds carved on open slopes by the action of turning ski-ers. Most new and intermediate ski-ers dislike moguls, especially on the steep slopes of 45° or over. However, moguls are a fact of life on the ski-slope, so you must be able to tackle them.

First, try and realise that if tackled correctly, moguls make turning easier. To use them you just obey two simple rules.

1. Turn on the top of the mogul.

2. Keep turning.

Fig. 18

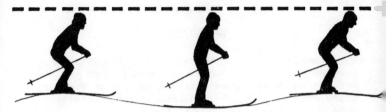

FLEXING THE KNEES TO ABSORB BUMPS.                     Fig. 19

Most moguls are on several descent lines. Although they look like a confused jumble of hillocks, there is a path through them, so find and use it. Do **not** traverse woefully up and down across the slope, looking for a flat bit. Come up on a mogul and TURN, down, up on a mogul and TURN.

The point is, that on top of a mogul your ski tips and tails are free, and only the centre, under your weight, is in contact with the snow. Turning is much easier as there is less resistance, for the tails are free to turn.

## THE MOGUL TURN

Turning on moguls does require a certain technique. The three turn points have been mentioned but are worth repeating.

1. Don't be afraid.

2. Turn on the top.

3. Keep turning.

Let us study the mogul turns in a typical situation. You have come down the piste through the trees, and arrived at the top right hand corner (looking down) of a well-moguled slope. You stop and quail. Others come bombing past you and lead out onto the slope. Study their routes and note the turning points.

The first turn on a mogul slope is always the most difficult. On the other hand, the spot to make it is usually the most obvious.

Traverse to the selected mogul, in the following position.

1. Skis slightly but not too far apart. You want good balance, but you **don't** want one ski either side of the mogul.

2. Weight evenly between the skis, **not** over the downhill one.

3. Lean well forward, and

4. Adopt a well flexed, knees-bent position.

Fig. 20

Ride out the bumps, flexing the knees and body as you rise and fall.

As you reach the turning point (the top of the mogul) your impetus and the upward pull will help unweight you forward. You now need to turn.

**Planting the Pole:** Plant the pole **down the side of the mogul,** level with your boot, and put some weight on it. This locks the shoulder down, at the turning point

**The Turn:** You are now riding up on the mogul, heading forward, both your shoulders are turning round the planted pole. You need to feel that you are swooping into the hollow.

Steer the ski tips down the mogul on the pole side, keeping the skis flat. Face down and out. This will swoop you right round into the hollow at the side of the mogul, and ready to traverse and turn on another one.

What you have done is this, you rode up onto the top of the lump, planted the pole, while flexed, unweighted forward and turned, slid down the side of the mogul and traversed away. It sounds easy if you say it quick!

That is the essence of the turn, but there are, as always, a few do's and dont's.

DO

1. Head downhill.
2. Turn quickly, after planting the pole on the side of the mogul.
3. Keep turning.
4. Turn on the top.
5. Keep flexed and lean forward.

DON'T

1. Lean backwards.
2. Plant the pole on top of the mogul—plant it **on the side.**
3. Let the legs get rigid, let them flex like a bed spring.
4. Let the ski tips cross.

## SPEED
If you go too fast into moguls you can fly into the air. Keep some speed on, but control it by running up the side of moguls and side-

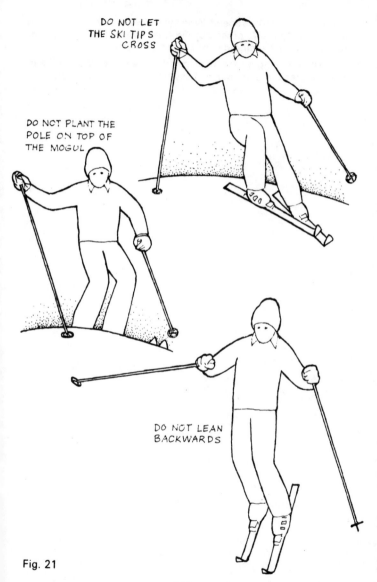

Fig. 21

slipping down to lose speed. When you have turned, edge the skis into the mogul and press out the turn. Aim for tight controlled turns, always heading downhill, and always turning.

Keep practising on mogul slopes. On the steep slopes, moguls are like steps in a staircase. They help you get down safely.

Chapter 9

# JET TURNS, AVALEMENT, WEDEL

## THE JET-TURN
The jet turn sounds terrific, and the person who named it deserves a medal, if only for making people nervous. However, it is a useful turn, an extension of the parallel, and especially useful if you get out of control on running moguls, or have to run down a slope, moguled or not, which is too narrow for an adequate traverse.

The two basic requirements for the jet turn are:

1. A backward-leaning, sitting down position.
2. The thrusting forward of the flattened parallel skis, across the fall-line.

   The jet-turn is induced by the following action:

1. Checking the slide by edging, and
2. Initiating the turn by turning the upper body, always keep the upper body across the fall-line.

What you are doing is slamming the skis across the slope in a braking movement, and turning by rebounding from the check thus induced.

**To learn the Turn:** Once you have a fair grasp of the parallel turn, find an even slope, and one that is, to your now practised eye, quite easy.

Head down or close to the fall-line, in a schuss, knees bent and weight well forward. Plant the pole, and as your legs pass the planted pole **shoot the legs forward,** and swing the skis into a turn **across the fall-line.** You will be leaning well back, on your pole, but as the pressure on the skis slows your momentum, your own weight brings you up and forward.

Repeat this movement to the other side and continue on down the slope. As you can see, for checking speed on a fast slope, the "jet turn" is a useful manoeuvre.

Now study the diagram (Fig. 22) on the two following pages, and then go out and run through the turn as fast as possible. Tried slowly it won't work.

SIDE SLIP
TAILS OF
SKIS

BEND FORWARD
PLANT THE POLE DOWNHILL
AND SUPPORT YOURSELF ON IT

Fig. 22

AS YOU PASS THE POLE
SHOOT THE LEGS FORWARD
AND SWING THE SKIS
ACROSS THE FALL LINE

## AVALEMENT

A stage further on, lies the turn the French call 'avalement', which is best employed by the rapidly improving intermediate skier, rather than the adequate beginner, for avalement is used to turn full speed among moguls. You need speed, and good flex since the avalement turn cannot be done without it.

**How to Start:**

1. Run a fairly straight traverse across the slope, and look for a big mogul slightly above (not below) your line.

2. Plant the **uphill** pole, to climb up this uphill mogul, knees well flexed.

3. Once on top, follow through with the downhill pole, planted as for a mogul turn on the downhill side, extend (Fig. 23), and swoop down into the dip. You are flexing and extending up and over the hump, thus ironing it out. This will be a tight turn and you can fall out of it unless you flex the knees and edge the skis during the turn, flattening them as you point them down the mogul, and flexing down for the next turn.

DO NOT

Plant the pole on top of the mogul. This gives you a turn, but sends you back on your tracks.

DO

Keep flexing the legs to absorb the bumps. With flexed knees you can push away at the snow to control your turn and speed. With locked straight legs, half your control is gone.

NOTICE HOW THE SKIER MAINTAINS THE SAME HEIGHT ACROSS THE MOGUL

Fig. 23

## WEDEL

A few years ago wedel was all the rage among intermediate and advanced skiers. People claimed to be doing wedel when they were doing all sorts of things, so let us start by defining wedel. Firstly, wedel is more than a turn. It is a method of descending a long even slope at speed and under control. In true wedel, your axis of descent is the fall-line, and **your ski tips stay on it**. Secondly, you **never** edge, or stem.

Since for true wedel, most methods of inducing a turn are discarded, how **do** you turn?

The method is called **counter-rotation**, ski tips facing one way, shoulders the opposite, and it works as follows:

1. Find an open, even, gentle slope.

2. Schuss directly down the fall-line, legs moderately flexed.

3. The arms are held out in front, fists at waist height.

4. Plant the pole, and swing the **tails** of the skis out across the fall-line, press out with the heels, this will check you.

5. While 4 is happening to the skis, swing the shoulders back at right angles to the fall-line and plant the pole again.

6. Plant the pole and swing the **tails** of the skis out across the fall-line, press out with the heels, this will check you, and repeat, repeat, repeat.

What you are after is a series of rythamic even swings and checks as close to the fall-line as possible.

These two turns Jet and avalement, and wedel, all take practice. They are refinements of parallel ski-ing and practicing them will improve your overall technique.

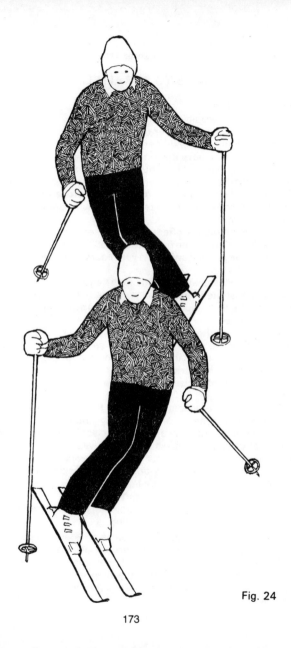

Fig. 24

## Chapter 10

## AIDS TO PARALLELING

### SKI-EVOLUTIF

It would be impossible to conclude a book on parallel ski-ing without including a chapter on ski-evolutif, a process designed entirely to teach the beginner to parallel.

Many ski-ers believe that once you have learnt to induce a turn by stemming, you will continue to do so, however much you try not to, and never do a pure parallel turn. The short ski, evolutif, or GLM method attempts to overcome this by proceeding straight to paralleling, and avoids such techniques as the snow plough turn, and the stem.

Most Alpine resorts offer ski-evolutif, and the method is quite simple. You start on the first day with skis about one metre long, and learn the parallel swing. As your course proceeds, so your ski length increases.

The method is geared directly to the equipment and cannot be fully demonstrated here. It is much easier to turn on short skis, and once the techniques are grasped, it can be applied as the skis are lengthened.

So, if you get the chance to START ski-ing on the ski-evolutif method, then we recommend you do so.

However, if you are into your second or third season and just about to grasp the parallel turn, then we think you should not change skis in mid-piste, but work to refine and improve your technique.

There are, in practice, two snags. Firstly, ski-evolutif is not available everywhere, and secondly, many ski shops are becoming reluctant to swap a whole classful of skis over every couple of days, as the class itself improves.

However, there is no doubt that evolutif works. If you can find it, take it. Even take private lessons on evolutif skis, and then apply the techniques on your normal skis, when practising later.

However, the recreational skier's holiday is of limited duration, and if any method can be found to hasten the advancement of his ski-ing ability, then it is worth trying.

Finally, even when you have become an adequate parallel ski-er, never neglect the basics. Concentrate always on refining your techniques, and learn to cope with the endless variations in snow conditions, crust, ice, powder, or the deep heavy stuff—at least by now you are off the nursery slopes and the mountains are open to you—and good luck!

IN SKI EVOLUTIF
THE BEGINNER
STARTS TO
PARALLEL BY
USING FIRSTLY
VERY SHORT SKIS
AND THEN
PROGRESSIVELY
LONGER SKIS

Fig. 25

# GLOSSARY OF TERMS

It helps to know what people are talking about!

| | |
|---|---|
| Bindings: | The metal attachments that clamp the boot to the ski. |
| Bindings, step-in | A modern binding that works by simply stepping down into the gap between heel and toe plate. |
| Bindings, plate | A modern full-foot binding with multi-direction release. |
| Edges: | The metal strips that run along the outer, underside edge of the ski. They should be complete and sharp. |
| 'Edging': | Turning the knees and ankles into the slope, to lift the flat bottom of the ski off the ground, and rest the weight on the edge; used in climbing, side skidding. |
| Fall-line: | The straight, shortest route down a slope is the 'Fall-line'. |
| Flo-fit': | A type of boot padding that expands and contracts with the warmth of the foot. |
| G.L.M. | Graduated Length Method. U.S. term for ski évolutif –- see below. |
| Instructor: | Ski-lehrer (German); Monitèur (French); Instructtore (Italian). |
| Langlauf: | Cross-country ski-ing, usually on special narrow skis, also called Nordic or 'ski de fond' (Fr.). |
| Moguls: | Bumps! A slope formed into bumps by the criss-cross tracks of ski-ers is called a 'mogul slope'. |
| Parallel: | Ski-ing and turning with the skis close together — a very attractive style of ski-ing. |
| Piste: | The prepared ski track, or route down a mountain. |
| Plough: | Putting the tips of the skis together by forcing heels out and knees together, used for slowing, stopping and turning, i.e., 'snow-plough' turn. |
| Powder snow: | The ideal soft, light snow, usually found off the piste. |
| Ski-évolutif: | A method of teaching ski-ing by starting with short skis and gradually increasing the length (also G.L.M.). |

| | |
|---|---|
| Side-stepping: | Climbing a slope on skis by 'edging' the skis and stepping up sideways. |
| Side-slipping: | A method of losing height while traversing, by letting the skis flatten and slip down the slope. |
| Slalom: | Coming down a slope in a series of wide turns, always made around markers. |
| Schuss: | Heading straight down a slope or piste — 'straight schuss'. |
| Ski: Uphill ski: | The ski closest to the slope. Uphill ski is usually held a little ahead of the downhill one. |
| Ski: Downhill Ski: | The ski farthest from the slope. 'Uphill' and 'Downhill' ski usually replace 'left' and 'right' in practice. |
| Salopettes: | A ski overall, consisting of trousers and bib. |
| Traversing: | Running across a slope, or across the fall-line, to turn at either side of the slope. |
| Waxes: | Preparations used on the bottoms of skis to help control movement, or avoid the build-up of snow on the ski. |